TURN MY MOURNING

into

dancing

*Primary Sources from the Henri J. M. Nouwen Archives
and Research Collection, John M. Kelly Library,
University of St. Michael's College*

INTRODUCTION

CHAPTER ONE

CHAPTER TWO

"On Departure" [between 1966–1971?], Manuscript Series.

"Spiritual Living and Ministry," 1991, transcript of sound
     recording, Manuscript Series.

"Deepening a Prayer Life," tape from talk given at Scarritt-Bennett
     Center, Nashville, February 8, 1991, Sound Recordings Series.

These sources are preserved in the Henri J. M. Nouwen Archives.
Further enquiries may be directed to Gabrielle Earnshaw, Archivist
at nouwen.archives@utoronto.ca. For more information, please visit
https://henrinouwen.org/.

CONTENTS

ACKNOWLEDGMENTS

Many thanks to Maureen Wright and Sue Mosteller at the Henri Nouwen Literary Centre and Gabrielle Earnshaw at The Henri J. M. Nouwen Archives and Research Collection, John M. Kelly Library, University of St. Michael's College in Toronto. It almost goes without saying that this book would not have come into being without them. Thanks also to John Mogabgab for his wonderful encouragement and to Robert Jonas for permission to share his story.

PREFACE

"It won't be enough," I decided early on, *"to visit only the* archives." To compile *Turn My Mourning into Dancing* would require my going deeper.

I would, of course, sort through the hundreds of pages of lecture notes and sermon transcripts that Henri Nouwen had left behind in shelved archive boxes. That went without saying. And I had every confidence that the files of unpublished writings of the late priest and author would yield ample material for a book. Decades of reading Nouwen's books on the spiritual life and ministry in a needy world had demonstrated his concern for prayer and his insight into human nature. That much I knew. But I wanted to gain also a greater sense of the person. As I worked with his archived files, I wanted to absorb more of the pastoral presence behind the jotted pages and typewritten notes.

That opportunity came serendipitously. My friend, John Mogabgab, Henri's assistant during his years at Yale Divinity School and editor of the esteemed journal *Weavings*, suggested that I also visit Daybreak, the community that serves the profoundly disabled where Henri spent his final years as pastor. Because the archives sit within easy driving distance of Daybreak, the way seemed clear. I would spend the days of that week in the John M. Kelly library of St. Michael's College in Toronto. And then spend the evenings at Daybreak, talking with Henri's associates, getting to know the community members, eating dinner with the "core members" and their assistants, even stay in the Cedars, a combination house and library that Henri himself founded, lived in, and used for writing.

I learned much in those moments about the man behind the words, even from the moment I stepped off the plane. Kathy, Henri's secretary for the last years of his life, met me at the airport to drive me to Daybreak; she stood with a sign that read "Daybreak Community welcomes Timothy." And welcome me they did. Sue Mosteller, Henri's executrix, and countless other members of the community welcomed me into their morning worship services, group homes, evening meals, and spur-of-the-moment conversations.

Kathy and Sue and others gave me glimpses into a man with a heart that constantly reached out to hurting souls. He lived with immense and inspired energy, I learned. He received calls from people with deep needs constantly—people with no prior relationship to Henri that most public figures would ask to be shielded from.

And the community itself! Years before, Henri had resigned from Harvard to spend a sabbatical year writing in

Trosly-Breuil, France, in the original community of L'Arche that served people who had cognitive and physical disabilities. He felt so at home there that in 1986 he accepted an invitation to become pastor for the L'Arche community of Daybreak near Toronto, Canada. His finding Daybreak, he and so many of his friends said, represented a homecoming. This professor who taught some of the nation's brightest and most articulate divinity students—with stints at Notre Dame, Yale, and Harvard—spent the final years of his life ministering profoundly through his gentle (if sometimes intense) presence and his simple, pastoral words of blessing. His writing continued, of course, and his influence only grew in one of the paradoxes that truly great figures so frequently live out.

Since Henri Nouwen's death in 1996, interest in his writings has only gathered momentum. The key has to do, I believe, with far more than his sometime artful turns of phrase or his striking accomplishments. More than anything, I believe, the continued interest grows out of who he was—a heart broken before God and opened for his fellow friends and readers. Henri was complex and unfinished; he knew it well and did not pretend otherwise. But still, he also knew, there was ministering to be done. Suffering to care for. Hope to bring to bear in life's dark places.

All this, I hope the reader will discover, informed the sermons and lectures and scribbled notes that comprised and fed into this book. *Turn My Mourning into Dancing* offers yet more glimpses from the pen—and the life—of this slightly stooped, always passionate preacher of spirituality. As we learn from this chronicler of the possibilities of a human life lived vibrantly with God, may our sorrows also turn to expectancy and even joy.

Timothy Jones

INTRODUCTION

HOPE IN OUR HURTING WORLD

This afternoon my good friend Jonas called, his voice trembling, shock muting his voice. His daughter, he told me, had died four hours after birth. "Margaret and I and our three-year-old son, Sam, had so been looking forward to the new baby," he said. "She had been born early in an emergency C-section, but still, it looked as if she would come through." The vital signs soon told them that Rebecca could not live long.

In the intensive care unit, Jonas and Margaret held the tiny life in their arms. Then it was all over. Jonas said a prayer for the baby, he told me, and made the sign of the cross.

I was struck by what Jonas said next. "Driving away from the hospital, I kept telling God, 'You have given us Rebecca and now I return her to you. But I know a beautiful future is being cut off. It hurts so much to lose her. I feel such emptiness.'"

I searched for the right words. What could I say? I did not want to interfere with Jonas's grieving. But I also knew that

Jonas would not have to face this grief without consolation. "Rebecca," I said, "is your daughter—yours and Margaret's. She always will be. Sam will always have a sister. Rebecca was given only a few hours, but they were not futile. Your prayers are not in vain. She lives now in God's eternal embrace."

It was a long conversation. I know my words gave only modest comfort. More than anything Jonas and I wanted to hug one another and cry. How important did our friendship seem at such a time!

And I wondered again, as perhaps we all wonder when grief hits hard and hurts us deeply: Why did such a thing happen? To reveal God's glory? To remind us of the fragility of life? Or perhaps to deepen the faith of those who carry on? It is hard to answer yes when everything seems so dark.

When I think of Margaret and Jonas holding tiny Rebecca in their arms, I think also of Jesus' own mother. So often paintings and statues depict her holding her Son's limp, lifeless body on her lap. She was not bereft, not left without hope, but what pain she endured to watch her Son die on a cross! And as I think of my friends Margaret and Jonas, I feel moved to pray.

The hardships we all endure require more than words, of course, even spiritual words. Eloquent phrases cannot soothe our deep pain. But we do find something to lead and guide us through. We hear an invitation to allow our mourning to become a place of healing, and our sadness a way through pain to dancing. Who is it Jesus said would be blessed? "Those who mourn" (Matt. 5:4). We learn to look fully into our losses, not evade them. By greeting life's pains with something other than denial, we may find something unexpected. By inviting God into our difficulties, we ground life—even its sad moments—in joy and hope. When we stop grasping our lives, we can finally be given more than we could ever grab for ourselves. And we learn the way to a deeper love for others.

How can we learn to live this way? Many of us are tempted to think that if we suffer, the only important thing is to be relieved of our pain. We want to flee it at all costs. But when we learn to move through suffering, rather than avoid it, then we greet it differently. We become willing to let it teach us. We even begin to see how God can use it for some larger end. Suffering becomes something other than a nuisance or curse to be evaded at all costs, but a way into deeper fulfillment. Ultimately mourning means facing what wounds us in the presence of One who can heal.

This is not easy, of course. This dance will not usually involve steps that require no effort. We may need to practice. With that in mind, this little book shows five movements of a life grounded in God. These will not make the pain disappear. They will not mean we can expect to avoid shadowed valleys and long nights. But these steps in the dance of God's healing choreography let us move gracefully amid what would harm us and find healing as we endure what could make us despair. We can ultimately find a healing that lets our wounded spirits dance again, that lets them dance unafraid of suffering and even death because we learn to live with lasting hope.

Five Movements Through Hard Times

1

FROM OUR LITTLE SELVES
TO A LARGER WORLD

When I came to Daybreak, the community of ministry to disabled people where I have been pastor, I was experiencing a great deal of personal pain. My many years in the world of academics, my travels among the poor in Central America, and later, my speaking around the world about what I had seen, left me deflated. My schedule kept me running hard and fast. Rather than providing an escape from my own inner conflicts, my scurrying from speaking engagement to speaking engagement only intensified my inner turmoil. And because of my schedule, I could not fully face my pain. I carried on with the illusion that I was in control, that I could avoid what I did not want to face within myself and in the world around me.

But when I arrived, I witnessed the enormous suffering of

the mentally and physically handicapped persons living here. I came gradually to see my painful problems in a new light. I realized they formed part of a much larger suffering. And I found through that insight new energy to live amid my own hardship and pain.

I realized that healing begins with our taking our pain out of its diabolic isolation and seeing that whatever we suffer, we suffer it in communion with all of humanity, and yes, all of creation. In so doing, we become participants in the great battle against the powers of darkness. Our little lives participate in something larger.

I also found something else here: people asking not so much "How can I get rid of my suffering?" but "How can I make it an occasion for growth and insight?" Among these people, most of whom cannot read, many of whom cannot care for themselves, among men and women rejected by a world that values only the whole and bright and healthy, I saw people learning how to make the connection between human suffering and God's suffering. They helped me to see how the way through suffering is not to deny it, but to live fully in the midst of it. They were asking how they could turn pain from a long interruption into an opportunity.

How do we make such connections ourselves? How do we make this shift from evading our pain to asking God to redeem and make good use of it?

Counting Our Losses

An early step in the dance sounds very simple, though often will not come easily: we are called to grieve our losses. It seems paradoxical, but healing and dancing begin with looking squarely at what causes us pain. We face the secret losses that have paralyzed us and kept us imprisoned in denial or shame or guilt. We do not nurse the illusion that we can hopscotch our way through difficulties. For by trying to hide parts of our story from God's eye and our own consciousness, we become judges of our own past. We limit divine mercy to our human fears. Our efforts to disconnect ourselves from our own suffering end up disconnecting our suffering from God's suffering for us. The way out of our loss and hurt is in and through. When Jesus said, "For I have come to call not the righteous but sinners" (Matt. 9:13), he affirmed that only those who can face their wounded condition can be available for healing and enter a new way of living.

Sometimes we need to ask ourselves just what our losses are. Doing so reminds us how real the experience of loss is. Perhaps you know what it is to have a parent die. How well I remember the grief I felt after my mother's illness and death. We may experience the death of a child or of friends. And we lose people, sometimes just as painfully, through misunderstanding, conflict, or anger. I may expect a friend to visit, but he does not come. I speak to a group and expect a warm reception, but no one really seems to respond. Someone may take from us a job, a career, a good name.

We may watch hopes flicker through growing infirmity, or dreams vanish through the betrayal of someone we trusted for a long time. A family member may walk out in anger, and we wonder if we have failed. Sometimes our sense of loss feels large indeed: I read the newspaper and find things only worse than the day before. Our souls grow sad because of poverty or the destruction of so much natural beauty in our world. And we may lose meaning in our lives, not only because our hearts become tired, but also because someone ridicules long-cherished ways of thinking and praying. Our convictions suddenly seem old-fashioned, unnecessary. Even our faith seems shaky. Such are the potential disappointments of any life.

Typically we see such hardship as an obstacle to what we think we should be—healthy, good-looking, free of discomfort. We consider suffering as annoying at best, meaningless at worst. We strive to get rid of our pains in whatever way we can. A part of us prefers the illusion that our losses are not real, that they come only as temporary interruptions. We thereby expend much energy in denial. "They should not prevent us from holding on to the real thing," we say to ourselves.

Several temptations feed this denial. Our incessant busyness, for example, becomes a way to escape what must some days be confronted. The world in which we live lies in the power of the Evil One, and the Evil One would prefer to distract us and fill every little space with things to do, people to meet, business to accomplish, products to be made. He does not allow any space for genuine grief and mourning. Our busyness becomes a curse, even while we think it provides us with relief from the pain inside. Our over-packed lives serve only to keep us from facing the inevitable difficulty that we all, at some time or another, must face.

The voice of evil also tries to tempt us to put on an invincible front. Words such as *vulnerability, letting go, surrendering, crying, mourning,* and *grief* are not to be found in the devil's dictionary. Someone once said to me, "Never show your weakness, for you will be used; never be vulnerable, for you will get hurt; never depend on others, for you will lose your freedom." This might sound very wise, but it does not echo the voice of wisdom. It mimics a world that wants us to respect without question the social boundaries and compulsions that our society has defined for us.

Facing our losses also means avoiding a temptation to see life as an exercise in having needs met. We are needy people, of course: We want attention, affection, influence, power. And our needs seem never to be satisfied. Even altruistic actions can get tangled with these needs. Then, when people or circumstances do not fulfill all of our needs, we withdraw or lash out. We nurse our wounded spirits. And we become even needier. We crave easy assurances, ignoring anything that would suggest another way.

We also like easy victories: growth without crisis, healing

without pains, the resurrection without the cross. No wonder we enjoy watching parades and shouting out to returning heroes, miracle workers, and record breakers. No wonder our communities seem organized to keep suffering at a distance: People are buried in ways that shroud death with euphemism and ornate furnishings. Institutions hide away the mentally ill and criminal offenders in a continuing denial that they belong to the human family. Even our daily customs lead us to cloak our feelings and speak politely through clenched teeth and prevent honest, healing confrontation. Friendships become superficial and temporary.

The way of Jesus looks very different. While Jesus brought great comfort and came with kind words and a healing touch, he did not come to take all our pains away. Jesus entered into Jerusalem in his last days on a donkey, like a clown at a parade. This was his way of reminding us that we fool ourselves when we insist on easy victories. When we think we can succeed in cloaking what ails us and our times in pleasantness. Much that is worthwhile comes only through confrontation.

The way from Palm Sunday to Easter is the patient way, the suffering way. Indeed, our word *patience* comes from the ancient root *patior*, "to suffer." To learn patience is not to rebel against every hardship. For if we insist on continuing to cover our pains with easy "Hosannas," we run the risk of losing our patience. We are likely to become bitter and cynical or violent and aggressive when the shallowness of the easy way wears through.

Instead, Christ invites us to remain in touch with the many sufferings of every day and to taste the beginning of hope and new life right there, where we live amid our hurts and pains and brokenness. By observing his life, his followers discover that when all of the crowd's "Hosannas" had fallen silent, when disciples and friends had left him, and after Jesus cried out, "My God, my God, why have you forsaken me?" then it was that the Son of Man rose from death. Then he broke through the chains of death and became Savior. That is the patient way, slowly leading me from the easy triumph to the hard victory.

I am less likely to deny my suffering when I learn how God uses it to mold me and draw me closer to him. I will be less likely to see my pains as interruptions to my plans and more able to see them as the means for God to make me ready to receive him. I let Christ live near my hurts and distractions.

I remember an old priest who one day said to me, "I have always been complaining that my work was constantly interrupted; then I realized that the interruptions were my work." The unpleasant things, the hard moments, the unexpected setbacks carry more potential than we usually realize. For the movement from Palm Sunday to Easter takes us from the easy victory built on small dreams and illusions to the hard victory offered by the God who waits to purify us by his patient, caring hand.

As I learned from my friends at Daybreak, at the center of our Christian faith we perceive a God who took on himself the burden of the entire world. Suffering invites us to place our hurts in larger hands. In Christ we see God suffering—for us. And calling us to share in God's suffering love for a hurting world. The small and even overpowering pains of our lives are intimately connected with the greater pains of Christ. Our daily sorrows are anchored in a greater sorrow and therefore a larger hope. Absolutely nothing in our lives lies outside the realm of God's judgment and mercy.

What Happens, What Doesn't

One of life's great questions centers not on what happens to us, but rather, how we will live in and through whatever happens. We cannot change most circumstances in our lives. I am white, middle class, and I have a good education. I have not always made conscious decisions about these things. Very little of what I have lived, in fact, has to do with what I have decided—whom I have known, where I came into the world, what personality tendencies have taken hold.

Our choice, then, often revolves around not what has happened or will happen to us, but how we will relate to life's turns and circumstances. Put another way: will I relate to my life resentfully or gratefully? Think of this example: You and I have crashed into one another on the highway. For me it might create not only serious injury, but also bitter resentfulness. I may drag through life, saying, "The accident changed everything. Now I am broken, and life is hard." You may suffer the same hardship, but say, "Might this moment serve as a call to another way of life? Might it be an opportunity to master something new, a chance to make my brokenness serve as a witness to others?"

The losses may be nonnegotiables. But we have a choice: how do we live these losses? We are called time and again to discover God's Spirit at work within our lives, within us, amid even the dark moments. We are invited to choose life. A key in understanding suffering has to do with our not rebelling at the inconveniences and pains life presents to us.

Joining in the Larger Dance

Mourning makes us poor; it powerfully reminds us of our smallness. But it is precisely here, in that pain or poverty or awkwardness, that the Dancer invites us to rise up and take the first steps. For in our suffering, not apart from it, Jesus enters our sadness, takes us by the hand, pulls us gently up to stand, and invites us to dance. We find the way to pray, as the psalmist did, "You have turned my mourning into dancing" (Ps. 30:11), because at the center of our grief we find the grace of God.

And as we dance, we realize that we don't have to stay on the little spot of our grief but can step beyond it. We stop centering our lives on ourselves. We pull others along with us and invite them into the larger dance. We learn to make room for others—and the Gracious Other in our midst. And when we become present to God and God's people, we find our lives richer. We come to know that all the world is our dance floor. Our step grows lighter because God has called out others to dance as well.

A friend wrote me a letter to recount his discovery. He had decided to spend the week following Christmas with his father, who suffers from Alzheimer's disease. One morning, when he met his father at the day program in which he takes part, he found him very anxious and agitated. His father was worrying that his own mother, who had died long before my friend was born, needed his help. The worries were clearly an expression of a deep anguish that he could not express directly.

My friend took his father for a drive for more than an hour through the countryside. Very few words were spoken between them, but my friend noticed how his father's anxiety diminished, and he became more relaxed. After not speaking for nearly an hour, the father turned, looked directly at his son, and said, "Well, we haven't had such a good visit in a long time." The son laughed and realized that his father was right. Anguish had become peace; loss had become gain. Even the silence between them held healing. So much of our movement through suffering has to do with such unexpected moments. Moments that come as gifts amid our waiting or struggling. Moments that often have much to do with the people God puts in our path.

We do not, then, attempt our movement from our little lives into God's larger grace by simple resolve or lonely effort. When our needs lead us to grab desperately for a place, when our unhealed wounds determine the atmosphere around us, we become anxious. But then we let our hurt remind us of our need for healing. As we dance and walk forward, grace provides the ground on which our steps fall. Prayer puts us in touch with the God of the Dance. We look beyond our experience of sadness or loss by learning to receive an all-embracing love, a love that meets us in everyday moments.

And so we wait patiently, if the situation requires it, watching for gifts to come where we are. Look at the wonderful, exuberant flowers painted by the famous Dutch artist Vincent van Gogh. What grief, what sadness, what melancholy he experienced in his difficult life! Yet what beauty, what ecstasy! Looking at his vibrant paintings of sunflowers, who can say where the mourning ends and the dance begins? Our glory is hidden in our pain, if we allow God to bring the gift of himself in our experience of it. If we turn to God, not rebelling against our hurt, we let God transform it into greater good. We let others join us and discover it with us.

Gratitude at the Core

Recently a friend left the Daybreak community to assume the leadership of another similar community. Her years of faithful self-giving were marked by moments of great joy as well as moments of great sorrow. She had developed warm and deep friendships, accomplished many beautiful things, and assumed roles of leadership. She had also experienced failure and disappointment because some of those long relationships had been broken along the way and at the end. During the months before she left, my friend, together with other members of their community, were heard to say things like, "We are thankful for all the good things that have happened, for all the friendships we have developed, for all the hopes that have been realized. We simply have to try to accept the painful moments."

Listening to comments like these, I began to wonder just exactly what it would mean for my friend and for the community members to choose to be grateful for all that happened to them in their beloved fellowship. How could their gratitude help them enter more fully into a dance of healing and a celebration of joy? Perhaps nothing helps us make the movement from our little selves to a larger world than remembering God in gratitude. Such a perspective puts God in view in all of life, not just in the moments we set aside for worship or spiritual disciplines. Not just in the moments when life seems easy.

If God is found in our hard times, then all of life, no matter how apparently insignificant or difficult, can open us to God's work among us. To be grateful does not mean repressing our remembered hurts. But as we come to God with our hurts—honestly, not superficially—something life changing can begin slowly to happen. We discover how God is the One who invites us to healing. We realize that any dance of celebration must weave both the sorrows and the blessings into a joyful step.

I once saw a stonecutter remove great pieces from a huge rock on which he was working. In my imagination I thought *That rock must be hurting terribly. Why does this man wound the rock so much?* But as I looked longer, I saw the figure of a graceful dancer emerge gradually from the stone, looking at me in my mind's eye and saying, "You foolish man, didn't you know that I had to suffer and thus enter into my glory?" The mystery of the dance is that its movements are discovered in the mourning. To heal is to let the Holy Spirit call me to dance, to believe again, even amid my pain, that God will orchestrate and guide my life.

We tend, however, to divide our past into good things to remember with gratitude and painful things to accept or forget. This way of thinking, which at first glance seems quite natural, prevents us from allowing our whole past to be the source from which we live our future. It locks us into a self-involved focus on our gain or comfort. It becomes a way to categorize, and in a way, control. Such an outlook becomes another attempt to avoid facing our suffering. Once we accept this division, we develop a mentality in which we hope to collect more good memories than bad memories, more things to be glad about than things to be resentful about, more things to celebrate than to complain about.

Gratitude in its deepest sense means to live life as a gift to be received thankfully. And true gratitude embraces all of life: the good and the bad, the joyful and the painful, the holy and the not-so-holy. We do this because we become aware of God's life, God's presence in the middle of all that happens.

Is this possible in a society where joy and sorrow remain radically separated? Where comfort is something we not only expect, but are told to demand? Advertisements tell us that we cannot experience joy in the midst of sadness. "Buy this," they say, "do that, go there, and you will have a moment of happiness during which you will forget your sorrow." But is it not possible to embrace with gratitude all of our life and not just the good things we like to remember?

If mourning and dancing are part of the same movement of grace, we can be grateful for every moment we have lived. We can claim our unique journey as God's way to mold our hearts to greater conformity to Christ. The cross, the primary symbol of our faith, invites us to see grace where there is pain; to see resurrection where there is death. The call to be grateful is a call to trust that every moment can be claimed as the way of the cross that leads to new life. When Jesus spoke to his disciples before his death and offered them his body and blood as gifts of life, he shared with them everything he had lived—his joy as well as his pain, his suffering as well as his glory—and enabled them to move into their own mission in deep gratitude. Day by day we find new reasons to believe that nothing will separate us from the love of God in Christ.

Of course, it is easy for me to push the bad memories under the rug of my consciousness and think only about the good things that please me. It seems to be the way to fulfillment. By doing so, however, I keep myself from discovering the joy beneath the sorrow, the meaning to be coaxed out of even painful memories. I miss finding the strength that becomes visible in my weakness, the grace God told Paul would be "sufficient for you, for power is made perfect in weakness" (2 Cor. 12:9).

Gratitude helps us in this dance only if we cultivate it. For gratitude is not a simple emotion or an obvious attitude. Living gratefully requires practice. It takes sustained effort to reclaim my whole past as the concrete way God has led me to this moment. For in doing so I must face not only today's hurts, but the past's experiences of rejection or abandonment or failure or fear. While Jesus told his followers that they were intimately related to him as branches are to a vine, they still needed to be pruned to bear more fruit (see John 15:1–5). Pruning means cutting, reshaping, removing what diminishes vitality. When we look at a pruned vineyard, we can hardly believe it will bear fruit. But when harvest comes, we realize that the pruning allowed the vines to concentrate their energy and produce more grapes.

Grateful people learn to celebrate even amid life's hard and harrowing memories because they know that pruning is no mere punishment, but preparation. When our gratitude for the past is only partial, our hope for the future can likewise never be full. But our submitting to God's pruning work will not ultimately leave us sad, but hopeful for what can happen in us and through us. Harvesttime will bring its own blessings.

I am gradually learning that the call to gratitude asks us to say, "Everything is grace." As long as we remain resentful about things we wish had not happened, about relationships that we wish had turned out differently, mistakes we wish we had not made, part of our heart remains isolated, unable to bear fruit in the new life ahead of us. It is a way we hold part of ourselves apart from God.

Instead, we can learn to see our remembered experience of our past as an opportunity for ongoing conversion of the heart. We let what we remember remind us of whose we are—not our own, but God's. If we are to be truly ready for a new life in the service of God, truly joyful at the prospect of God's unfolding vocation for our lives, truly free to be sent wherever God guides, our entire past, gathered into the spaciousness of a converted heart, must become the source of energy that moves us onward.

It was important, then, that the departure of my friend from our community be seen as a moment in which to gather up everything she had lived and say, "Thanks be to God." To recall her history with us also as God's journey alongside her would set her firmly on the path to her new calling.

When I think of my own pain, the personal turmoil and inner unrest that I felt when I came to Daybreak, I realize how

God graciously brought me not to a sheltered place, isolated from pain. On the contrary, nowhere can I better see hardship than among handicapped people who have suffered, not only the loss of their mental and even physical agility, but also of family support, educational opportunities, and the privileges of marriage and an independent life. I have been surrounded by people in great and inevitable need. And still, nowhere have I celebrated so much or so richly than among these men or women who have mourned over so many losses. When we celebrate together, we do not marshal degrees, prizes, promotions, or awards, but rather that the gift of life has revealed itself in the midst of all the losses.

The decorations, cards, candles, wrapped gifts—the hugs, smiles, and kisses—are all expressions of life and hope. When I am part of these celebrations, be they the small celebrations around the dinner table or larger ones in the chapel or our meeting hall, I marvel at the dance to which the Spirit has called us.

2

FROM HOLDING TIGHT
TO LETTING GO

For years I have loved watching trapeze artists. The love began when my then-eighty-nine-year-old father came for a visit. *Let's go to the circus*, we decided one day. That evening we watched five South African trapeze artists—three fliers and two catchers. They danced in the air! The fliers soared and all was dangerous until they found themselves caught by the strong hands of their partners. I told my father that I had always wanted to fly like that, that perhaps I had missed my calling!

I am constantly moved by the courage of my circus friends. At each performance they trust that their flight will end with their hands sliding into the secure grip of a partner. They also know that only the release of the secure bar allows them to move on with arcing grace to the next. Before they can be caught, they must let go. They must brave the emptiness of space.

Living with this kind of willingness to let go is one of the greatest challenges we face. Whether it concerns a person, possession, or personal reputation, in so many areas we hold on at all costs. We become heroic defenders of our dearly gained happiness. We treat our sometimes inevitable losses as failures in the battle of survival.

The great paradox is that it is in letting go, we receive. We find safety in unexpected places of risk. And those who try to avoid all risk, those who would try to guarantee that their hearts will not be broken, end up in a self-created hell. C. S. Lewis wrote in *The Four Loves*,

> To love at all is to be vulnerable. . . . If you want to make sure of keeping [your heart] intact, you must give your heart to no one, not even to an animal. Wrap it carefully round with hobbies and little luxuries; avoid all entanglements; lock it up safe in the casket of your selfishness. But in that casket—safe, dark, motionless, airless—it will change. It will not be broken—it will become unbreakable, impenetrable, irredeemable. . . . The only place outside of Heaven where you can be perfectly safe from the danger of love is Hell.[1]

In so many ways, the more we insist on control and the more we resist the call to hold our lives lightly, the more we have to deny the reality of our losses and the more artificial our existence becomes. Our belief that we should grasp tightly what we need provides one of the great sources of our suffering. But letting go of possessions and plans and people allows us to enter, for all its risks, a life of new, unexpected freedom.

How can we live with greater willingness to let go? Another step in turning our mourning into dancing has to do with not clutching what we have, not trying to reserve a safe place we can rest in, not trying to choreograph our own or others' lives, but to surrender to the God whom we love and want to follow. God invites us to experience our not being in control as an invitation to faith.

Life's Great Illusion

It is our great illusion that life is a property to be owned or an object to be grasped, that people can be managed or manipulated. We sometimes try to establish a logic by which things must happen the way we want. Even our dreams often reveal how deeply runs this illusion. When we cannot be conquering heroes by day, at least, we think we can by night. There we appear as a misunderstood genius or the rescuer recognized too late by those who criticized us.

This illusion sometimes puts us on the road to a frantic search for selfhood and self-fulfillment. We want to be "true to ourselves"—or at least to our self-made image. We become so concerned with our identity that we preoccupy ourselves with our own unique distinction. We worry about how we are doing in comparison with others. This is the illusion that sets us on the road to competition, rivalry, and even violence. For it makes us conquerors who will fight for our place in the world, even at the cost of others. This illusion leads some to nervous activism, propelled by the belief that anyone is only the results of his or her work. The same illusion leads others to introspection with the assumption that they are their own deepest feelings.

Awareness of how such illusions grip us often comes through a crisis or hardship. In the face of a great pain or inescapable grief, we realize how little we control our lives, how feebly our protests change reality. Something happens to make us realize we can let go of a cherished ambition, bid farewell to a friend, or accept an ailing body. We relinquish the hope of a marriage or career recognition that seems out of reach. We look in the mirror and admit that we are not strikingly handsome, not always the center of conversation at parties, not always brilliant. And we allow ourselves to remember that not only does life include losses, but in the end we will in some sense lose everything because we will, inevitably, die. At the same time, we sense that there may be more to life than life.

Such discoveries remind us of our humble place in the scheme of things. They keep us from self-aggrandizement. Perhaps our need to hold life loosely is no more evident than in our daily relationships. Loving someone means allowing the other person to respond in ways you have no control over.

Every time you engage yourself in an intimate, loving way with someone else you become at least partly subject to the exhilaration of hearing another person's yes or the disappointment in his or her no. The more people you love, the more pain you may experience. For the great mystery of love is that while it can be received, it can also be rejected. Every time you love you enter into the risk of love.

Look at the story of Jesus in the last chapters of his life. Time and again in the New Testament we read the phrase "handed over" to refer to Jesus and his followers. God handed his Son over for our sins. Jesus no longer was the One who preached, spoke, healed, took the initiative. What was done, was done to him. He was spit on, led to the cross, flagellated, crucified. The Word, the One through whom all is created, now becomes a victim of his creation. That is what his death meant—being out of control, for our sakes, from great love.

Our pain and the suffering of the Lord are intimately connected. When we mourn, we die to something that gives us a sense of who we are. In this sense suffering always has much to do with the spiritual life. We surrender our striving denial of our limitations. We release our hold on a piece of our identity as a spouse, a parent, as a member of church, as a resident of a community or nation. We may even suffer for our faith. Jesus' first followers were handed over to persecution and death. And so we admit, not without many tears, that we sometimes must let go of what we hold very dear.

The burden of all this makes some cynical. "What is the

use?" they conclude. The temptation becomes to respond with a continuous complaint over our unfulfilled plans and programs. Grief becomes a chronic bitter taste.

Such realities drive others to desperate compulsions. By trying to alleviate their fears they increase them; they see more and more they must control, more and more to worry about. Such an insistence creates anxiety and agitation. Indeed, when our response to the world is driven by a drive to control and hold, we will never be satisfied. And since our needs will not be satisfied, we try harder and harder, until we are so concentrated on the means that we lose sight of the end. We become like someone who buys merchandise in great extravagance to deal with his fear of bankruptcy. And then he becomes so afraid of burglars that he cannot leave his house. He becomes trapped in his own fear, for all his attempts to escape it.

But the disciples of Jesus left their nets, the source of their economic security, and their families, the source of their emotional security, and followed One who promised to fulfill the deepest desires of their hearts. We know what that uncertainty feels like. And yet as we let go, we sense that something new, something wonderful can happen in its place.

Leaving Our Compulsions Behind

To be converted fully is to let God lead us out of our compulsions. It means that we admit how we give up ceaselessly trying to "fix" things. Freedom is the opposite of compulsive obsessions.

This is not easy, of course, mostly because intense needs motivate us. We feel lonely, for example, and thereby look—sometimes desperately—for someone who can take away the pain: a husband, wife, friend. We are all too ready to conclude that someone or something can finally take away our neediness.

In this way we come to expect too much from others. We become demanding, clingy, even violent. Relationships bend under a heavy weight because we lay exaggerated seriousness on them. We load our fellow human beings with immortal powers. In our worst moments, we make them objects to meet our expectations.

But whenever I choose other gods by making people or events the source of my joy, I find my sorrow only increases. When I demand from others what only God can give, I experience pain. A psalm in the Old Testament points to another way. "I say to the LORD, 'You are my Lord; I have no good apart from you'" (Ps. 16:2). Such a prayer arises out of the religious experience of a worshiper who knows himself to be sheltered by God's presence in the temple. The psalmist goes on to declare that God is his "portion," "cup," "lot." Such images hark back to earlier days in Israel when the Levites, God's servants, had no share in the other tribes' inheritance, but God was their "allotment" (Deut. 10:9). We see that the source of the psalmist's joy lies in a life lived in communion with God.

Many things in our lives matter intensely to us, of course. We cannot be whole without people to love and people who love us. We need food and places to live; we enjoy the company of a friend and the enjoyment of a book. But holding lightly means remembering that we are not what we acquire and accomplish as much as what we have received. The deepest joys come not from the money we earn, the friends we surround ourselves with, or the results we achieve; we are rather whom God made us to be in his infinite love. We are the gifts we are given, not just the conquests we wrest. As long as we keep running around, anxiously trying to affirm ourselves or be affirmed by others, we remain blind to One who has loved us first, dwells in our heart, and has formed our truest self. But we can also open our eyes. We can see a new way forward.

Moving Out of the House of Fear

Fear becomes a great obstacle in making this movement. If there is anything that has struck me while traveling throughout this country to speak and teach, it is that we are a fearful people. We dread physical need or discomfort. We fear for our safety and our jobs. We even grow fearfully suspicious of others and hoard our belongings. On the level of international relations, well-to-do countries, such as those where many of us live, build walls around our wealth so that no stranger can take it away from us. We build bombs to protect what we become convinced we must defend. But in a great irony, we thereby become captives of our own fears. Those who can make us afraid have power over us. Those who make us live in a house of fear ultimately take our freedom away.

When I lived among the poor in Latin America some years ago, I saw a people who lived in a different way. They had learned that fear need never rule. Amid torture and oppression and poverty were people living in gratitude and peace. I found less fear than in those living in countries such as ours, where so many possess so much. And I suddenly realized another aspect of oppression—the oppression not simply of the poor and downtrodden, but the paradoxical oppression of the ones in power. For the other side of the poverty of the nations of the South is the fear and guilt and loneliness of the North. The suffering of affluent countries such as ours—our anxiousness and loneliness—comes as a hidden consequence of our ignoring those who are less fortunate. It accompanies our unjust extravagance.

Wherever we live, the invitation of Christ beckons us to move out of the house of fear into the house of love: to leave our possessiveness for a place of freedom. The Word became flesh and pitched its tent among us so that God could dwell in the house of love among us. And Jesus tells us that he goes to the Father to prepare a house for us, that we can make our home in him as he does in us. "Where are you?" he asks. "Are you living in the place of love?"

Jesus speaks to us in the gospel with other strong words: "Do not be afraid." It is a word resounding through the whole gospel story: Gabriel said it to Zechariah before the birth of John the Baptist. Gabriel said it to Mary before the birth of Jesus. The angel declared it to the women at the tomb. And the Lord himself said it when he appeared to his disciples: "Do not be afraid" (Matt. 28:10). It is as though God is saying to us, "I am the God of love, a God who invites you to receive the gifts of joy and peace and gratitude the poor have discovered, and to let go of your fears so that you can start sharing what you hoard."

As we keep our eyes directed at the One who says, "Do not be afraid," we may slowly let go of our fear. We will learn to live in a world without zealously defended borders. We will be free to see the suffering of other people, free to respond not with defensiveness, but with compassion, with peace, with ourselves.

Converting Illusions Through Prayer

This movement comes about through prayer. In the Gospels we see, again and again, how Jesus goes off by himself—sometimes long before dawn—to pray. In prayer Jesus comes to understand, again and again, that it is the heavenly Father who sends him. It is God who gives him words to speak. He does not claim "prizes" of ministry for himself; rather he listens.

Only prayer allows us to hear another voice, to respond to the larger possibilities, to find a way out of our need to order and control. Then the questions that seem to shape our identity will not matter so much: Who says good things about me? Who doesn't? Who is my friend? My enemy? How many like me? As we make God the center of our lives, our sense of who we are will depend less on what others think of or say about us. We will cease being prisoners of the interpersonal.

Indeed, prayer shows us how to keep the interpersonal from becoming an idol. It reminds us that we learn to love only because we have glimpsed or sensed a first love, a supreme love. Here is the way to a love that transcends the interpersonal: "We love because he first loved us" (1 John 4:19). We find freedom as we are touched by that first love. For it is that love that will break us away from our alienation and separation. It is a love that can soothe our compulsions to hoard and pretend we can organize the future. It is a love that allows us to love others.

Prayer then becomes an attitude that sees the world not as something to be possessed but as a gift that speaks constantly of the Giver. It leads us out of the suffering that comes from insisting on doing things our way. It opens our hearts to receive. And prayer refreshes our memory about how other people reveal to us the gift of life.

When we pray, we admit that we don't know what God is going to do, but remember that we will never find out if we are not open to risks. We learn to stretch out our arms to the deep sea and the high heavens with an open mind and heart. In many ways prayer becomes an attitude toward life that opens itself up to a gift that is always coming. We find courage to let new things happen, things over which we have no control, but which now loom as less threatening.

And it is here that we find courage to face our human boundaries and hurts, whether our physical appearance, our being excluded by others, our memories of hurt or abuse, our oppression at the hands of another. As we find freedom to cry out in our anguish or protest someone's suffering, we discover ourselves slowly led into a new place. We become conditioned to wait for what we in our own strength cannot create or orchestrate. We realize that joy is not a matter of balloons and parties, not owning a house, or even having our children succeed in school. It has to do with a deep experience—an experience of Christ. In the quiet listening of prayer, we learn to make out the voice that says, "I love you, whoever else likes you or not. You are mine. Build your home in me as I have built my home in you."

The resurrected Jesus said to Peter, "I tell you, when you were younger, you used to fasten your own belt and to go wherever you wished. But when you grow old, you will stretch out your hands, and someone else will fasten a belt around you and take you where you do not wish to go." Jesus thereby, John tells us, indicated the kind of death by which Peter would glorify God. Then he said to him, "Follow me." (John 21:18–19). How radical this is! A psychologist would tell us, "When you were young someone else girded and guided you, but now that you are old you can go on your own power." But Jesus says that maturity means growing willingness to be led—even to places we might not eagerly choose. It is in that time and place of need that we turn to Another. We realize we cannot live without God. And all the recognitions and comforts of life take on a different cast.

This is difficult to say and easy to misunderstand; it can be perceived as masochism. But I am not talking about wanting to be punished, but rather about letting ourselves be stripped of our comfortable reliance on family, friends, success, health, and familiar ways of thinking. We can do so because in prayer we learn to trust that our nakedness will in the end be covered by kindness. Mourning not only means facing our losses; it also welcomes our losses as ways of following more radically the voice of love.

The gospel calls us continually to make Christ the source, the center, and the purpose of our lives. In him we find our home. In the safety of that place, our sadnesses can point us to God, even drive us into God's loving embrace. Here mourning our losses ultimately lets us claim our belovedness. Mourning opens us to a future we could not imagine on our own—one that includes a dance.

This is Jesus' way. The Man of Sorrows, acquainted with grief (Isa. 53:3), promised joy. "I have said these things to you so that my joy may be in you, and that your joy may be complete" (John 15:11). "You will weep and mourn," he said, "but your pain will turn into joy" (John 16:20).

Opening to a Surprising God

All this talk of letting go may challenge some long-held convictions. Even in our faith we may need to pry open our fingers and open our arms to a surprising God.

Some time ago I met a student who was sitting on the steps of a campus building, his head resting in his hands. "What's up?" I asked. "Or what's down?"

"Well," he said, "it all seems too much. There are too many courses, too many interesting things to do, too many choices to make. I feel like a kid in a candy store who has only a quarter and doesn't know how to spend it."

I think about my new friend because we often communicate in our schools, workplaces, and neighborhoods that if we just find enough time and energy we can conquer the field, conquer life. Even in our classes and lectures about God we are prone to reduce God to our preconceptions and systems. We are, after all, a little afraid of God. We want to love him, but we fence ourselves in and keep God at a distance. Our spiritual habits and customs become that fence. We say to God, in effect, that "if you want to come, you must use that old entrance, the old way."

But suffering frequently teaches us a lesson about the

incomprehensibility of God. Says God through Isaiah: "For as the heavens are higher than the earth, so are my ways higher than your ways and my thoughts than your thoughts" (Isa. 55:9).

This is ultimately a freeing word. It invites us not to make God conform to our desires, not to try to fix the rules. For we cannot, even should we try, get God in our grip and think, *Finally, now I understand.* Rather, after all the turmoil or the long night is over, we come with an empty hand, one we stretch out to God.

Our waiting on God, our asking questions about where he is taking us, can then cultivate in us a growing sensitivity to God's presence, as well as his absence. We learn to accept God's surprising ways and broken presence in our midst. We no longer secretly assume that if only we work hard enough at kingdom matters, or our jobs, or our church activities, surely we will finally experience God speaking to us. We find ourselves less often expecting God to come by our schedules or calculations.

In theology there is much talk of what God is, whom we understand God to be, how we perceive God to act. We speak of what we believe to be true. There will also be, if we do not insist on systematizing the Infinite and Ineffable, a lot of saying no—God is not just justice, not just love, not just freedom, not just this or that. God is greater than our hearts. We get enough glimpses to know that God surpasses our every ability to think or imagine.

At such moments, God asks us to jump from our secure perches, to stop calculating the risks. Jesus bids us, "Take up your cross, follow me, leave even your father and mother if you must. Don't insist on knowing exactly what comes next but trust that you are in the hand of God, who will guide your life." We can do so, because we are told again and again in Scripture, Don't be afraid. Give me a chance. I am your Savior, Guide, Friend, Bridegroom.

Letting Go of the Old

Such an openhanded posture may mean releasing our hold on certain prejudices. We are asked to surrender to a vision of God and God's people greater than we now know. We may have to release some boxes that can no longer hold the breadth of God's truth. We may need to develop another stance toward people we spend time with every day, or pass in our commutes to the office, or see on the news. Prayer, we may find, helps us see others as persons to be received, loved.

Jesus told a parable about a landowner who hired a series of workers. No matter at what point in the day he added the workers, at the end, "Each of them received the usual daily wage" (Matt. 20:9). The others, some of whom had labored from early in the morning, were furious when Jesus showed that God is free to forgive whom he wants to forgive. That God is not bound by the regulations made up by our own limited expectations. Jesus' hearers were even more furious when he showed so much sympathy for Mary Magdalene, a prostitute, and for Matthew, a tax collector.

As you enter into intimate communion with God, you enter into intimate communion with the people of God. Prayer is communion with God in the privacy of our own places. It is also communion with the people of God around the world and through the centuries. Such love overcomes the fear that separates us. Such love allows us to let go of our little fears.

This may seem difficult, but such love, as it works in us, ultimately offers us a way out of self-righteousness and oppression. It rescues us from the illusion that makes the rich think they know what is best for the poor, men think they know what is best for women, or White people think they know what is best for Black people. It saves us from the illusion of power that leads us to Auschwitz, Hiroshima, or Jonestown.

Looking for the Day

Such love also keeps our relinquishing of our illusion of control from becoming mere passivity. Letting go of our small vision of God or our prejudices does not mean we should not care passionately. Time and again in the Bible we see God's people actively working for God's new thing. Fighting for justice. Seeking the kingdom. The writer of the second letter of Peter speaks of our "waiting for and hastening the coming of the day of God" (2 Peter 3:12). That is a call to look, to keep our eyes open, to be awake, alert, and always watching. And so to be engaged in working for the good while we watch.

But part of our waiting and watching and serving has to do with first becoming seers, people who discern the coming of God into our midst and in our world. Is there a space in your life where the Spirit of God has a chance to speak or act or show up? To be contemplative means to peel off the blindfolds that keep us from seeing his coming in us and around us. It means to learn to listen in the spaces of quiet we leave for God and thereby know how better to relate to the world around us.

Recently I spent some time walking in New York City. I realized how most places are filled up with other things. So much is crowded into that place! We seem to have a fear of empty spaces. The philosopher Spinoza called this a *horror vacui*. We want to fill up what is empty. Our lives stay very full. And when we are not blinded by busyness, we fill our inner space with guilt about things of the past or worries about things to come. Perhaps part of our fear comes from the fact that an empty place means that something may happen to us that we cannot predict, that is new, that leads us to a place we might not want to go. I might not want to hear what God has to say.

Here is the place for cultivating an open heart. Discipline is the concentrated effort to create some space in our lives where the Spirit of God can touch us, guide us, speak to us, and lead us to places that are unpredictable, where we are no longer in control. Many spiritual-life writers speak of "attentiveness" to God. Attentiveness helps us look fully at God, to invite God in more completely. It leads us into the depths of God's healing mercies. This attention, writes Simone Weil,

> consists of suspending our thought, leaving it detached, empty, and ready to be penetrated by the object. . . . All wrong translations, all absurdities in geometry problems, all clumsiness of style, and all faulty connections of ideas in compositions and essays, all such things are due to the fact that thought has seized upon some idea too hastily, and being thus prematurely blocked, is not open to the truth. The cause is always that we have wanted to be too active; we have wanted to carry out a search. . . . We do not obtain the most precious gifts by going in search of them but by waiting for them.[2]

Discipline in this sense is not as we sometimes mean it—mastering the discipline of sociology, for example, or law or nursing. I am not talking about a body of material or a set of organizing principles and practices. Discipline, in the sense I mean, is to leave room in our hearts where we can listen to the Spirit of God in a life-changing way. We guard space in our lives to become sensitive and receptive to God's word. We find in those risky acts something wonderfully beyond what we could have done on our own, by ourselves, without God.

That is a lesson I learn over and over, again and again.

Ever since I paid that visit to the circus with my father, ever since I found myself captivated by the trapeze artists, I have joined their circus group every year for a week or so to travel with them. The leader recently said to me, "Henri, everyone applauds for me because when I do those leaps and backflips, they think I am the hero. But the real hero is the catcher. The only thing I have to do is stretch out my hands and trust, trust that he will be there to pull me back up."

We can say no less about the God who encircles our little lives and waits to catch us and hold us—in the hard junctures and the good, in the precarious moments and the times we soar. Someone within us and yet beyond us always makes that possible. Because of that our tight grip on life—its joys and even its sorrows—can loosen. We too can learn again to fly—to dance.

3

FROM FATALISM TO HOPE

Can you remember what you were doing a year ago today? What you were talking about? What made you angry or happy, anxious or confident? You may have a few vivid memories if something dramatic happened. But for most of us, what preoccupied us on that day has grown fuzzy or vanished from conscious memory.

Were I to ask you to go back three or four years, you would find it even harder to remember. Events that chained us to the TV might seem like flashes from the past. Some once-current issues have faded in urgency. We may hear only rarely or not at all from a colleague or friend who absorbed our attention.

Suddenly it can hit you how fleeting our existence is, how like water that we cannot hold in our hands. Recognizing this can fill us with sadness since it makes us realize that something of us is dying all the time. It may lead us to conclude that we should never expect much. It may make us forget that new possibilities almost always wait around the corner.

But while presidents and popes came and went, while wars exploded and came to an end, while some lost their jobs only later to have their talents recognized, while children grew sickly and later became sports heroes, while all this and more transpired, something was being formed that neither death nor illness could destroy. For those who have eyes to see and ears to hear, much in our fleeting lives is not passing but lasting, not dying but coming to life, not temporary but eternal. Amid the fragility of our lives, we have wonderful reason to hope.

Some call this hidden reality "grace," others "God's life in us," others still "the kingdom of God among us." Whatever the name you give, once you focus your eyes and ears on the precious center, you start to realize that all the torrents of time and circumstance that roll over it serve only to polish it into a precious, imperishable gift. Anyone who believes, Jesus reminds us, has eternal life (John 6:40). That is the enormous revolution, that in this fleeting, temporary world he comes to plant the seed of eternal life. In many ways that is what is meant by the term *the spiritual life*—the nurturing of the eternal amid the temporal, the lasting within the passing, God's presence in the human family. It is the life of the divine Spirit within us.

Become aware of this mysterious presence and life turns around. You sense joy even as others nurse complaints, you experience peace while the world conspires in war, and you find hope even when headlines broadcast despair. You discover a deep love even while the air around you seems pervaded by hatred.

The Lure of Fatalism

It does not always seem so simple, of course. Sometimes we forget to see the eternal in the midst of the temporary. Sometimes we see life's transitory quality as a cause for resignation.

Fatalism is the "acceptance of every event as inevitable," according to *Webster's* dictionary.[1] And such a view is more pervasive than we may realize. Albert Nolan writes in *Jesus before Christianity,* "Fatalism is the prevailing attitude of most people, most of the time. It finds expression in statements like, 'Nothing can be done about it'; 'You can't change the world'; 'You must be practical and realistic'; . . . 'You must accept reality.'"[2] A fatalistic person says, "What is the use? We will lose in the end. We are victimized by fate." This easily leads to resentment, bitterness, hopelessness, despair.

Fatalism afflicts us in many ways. It affects our relationships. We use labels and categories that prevent us from expecting anything new from each other. "That is how she is," someone says, assuming that settles the matter. "That behavior is typical of him," we mumble. Or the place where we work or the institutions with which we deal may impress on us the same thinking: "That is how things are done here."

And so we give up trying to do something different, even if we see a better way. Just as bad, we may settle for being treated in hurtful or harmful ways. We allow others to abuse us not out of our humility, but because we despair that anything might be different. We see fate—or habitual mistreatment—as an anonymous power that keeps us imprisoned.

It affects our response to global issues of poverty and war and oppression. "This social problem is too complex for me to get involved," people say. "How could I possibly make a difference?" And many people caught in poverty or other social distress can hardly believe things could get better. They may give up trying to break out of their socioeconomic prison. They lose a dream for a more just way of life.

All these and many other forms of fatalism reveal our hidden despair. They suggest that fate is an anonymous power that keeps us imprisoned. The side effects plague us: Fatalism may make us dependent on routines, on actions that we would feel urgency to change if we examined them. We may settle for finding satisfaction in dysfunctional, painful places, growing attached to our complaints, symptoms, addictions.

One of the most insidious aspects of fatalism has to do with how it leads us to resist healing. We become hostage to a discouragement that insists that nothing more can be done. Fatalism reinforces our tenacious grasp on the old. We become stubbornly unwilling to consider anything outside our narrow experience. Fatalism can lead to depression, despair, even suicide.

The story in John's Gospel of the sick man at the pool of Bethesda shows this resistance; Jesus asks the man, "Do you want to be made well?" The poor man says he has tried to get into the healing waters, but he always manages to get in too late. His complaint becomes both an explanation of his condition and evidence of his dejection. For alongside the desire for healing now resides a sense of futility that makes him hold back around Jesus. His frustrated efforts have so discouraged him that he seems almost to have given up hoping and wanting. Why else would Jesus ask him, "Do you want to be made well?" (See John 5:1–9.)

Faith Against Fatalism

To say of a situation, "It is out of my hands," can represent a fatalistic remark or a mark of faith. Faith, after all, might seem to major in resignation; it too asks us to say, "I give myself into hands beyond my own." But faith looks very different from fatalism. It is its radical opposite. Rather than displaying passive resignation, faith leads us to hopeful willingness. A person of faith is willing to let new things happen and shoulder responsibilities that arise from unheard-of possibilities. Trust in God allows us to live with active expectation, not cynicism. When we view life as a gift, as something given to us by a loving God, not wrestled by us from an impersonal fate, we remember that at the heart of reality rests the love of

God itself. This means that faith creates in us a new willingness to let God's will be done.

The word so often translated *faith* in the New Testament comes from an ancient word that literally means "trust." Faith is the deep confidence that God is good and that God's goodness somehow triumphs. Faith is that intimate, personal trust by which you say, "I commend myself into your strong, loving hands." It is not hard to see how genuine hope is different from optimism. We are not talking about a sunny disposition that makes us believe things will be better tomorrow. An optimist says, "The war will be over; your wounds will be healed; the depression will go away; all will be better soon." The optimist may be right, but unfortunately he or she may also be wrong. For none of us can control our circumstances.

No, hope does not come from positive predictions about the state of the world, any more than does faith. Nor does hope depend on the ups and downs of our life's particulars. Hope rather has to do with God. We have hope and joy in our faith because we believe that, while the world in which we live is shrouded in darkness, God has overcome the world. "In the world," said Jesus, "you face persecution. But take courage; I have conquered the world!" (John 16:33). We follow One who is not limited or defeated by the world's sufferings.

Jesus would ask us: "Do you believe? Do you trust? Do you trust that God loves you so much that he wants to give you only life?" When I try to answer, I realize how far I have to go. Much in me says, "I want to be sure that there are certain things in place before I take the leap of faith." Every time I try to trust, I realize how many little conditions I put on trust. Every time I trust more, I see how deep is my resistance. And how many more levels I find that faith has not penetrated! We don't know how many levels there are. But our lives are renewed every time we trust more. We take a leap of faith and trust only to see the next layer of possibility.

Hope does not mean that we will avoid or be able to ignore suffering, of course. Indeed, hope born of faith becomes matured and purified through difficulty. The surprise we experience in hope, then, is not that, unexpectedly, things turn out better than expected. For even when they do not, we can still live with a keen hope. The basis of our hope has to do with the One who is stronger than life and suffering. Faith opens us up to God's sustaining, healing presence. A person in difficulty can trust because of a belief that something else is possible. To trust is to allow for hope.

Which also means that to trust is not always to demand specifics of what will transpire. God wants us to know life—but what that actually means is open-ended. God wants us to experience healing, but how can we know precisely what healing will always look like? God wants to bring us to a new place of faithfulness, but how and through what means? We don't have to decide everything or know everything or even glimpse much at all; if we try too hard to figure it all out, we lose a trusting spirit. A person of faith learns to trust so much that the outcome of the trust is given into the hands of the

One in whom the trust is placed. We let God work out some details that we feel tempted to know or control but ultimately cannot.

This kind of attention to the eternal in our everyday does not strain our hearts. It does not major on brawny striving. It has more to do with attention to God than perfection, with a desire to see God even amid our great weakness. Writes Simone Weil,

> Most often attention is confused with a kind of muscular effort. If one says to one's pupils, "Now you must pay attention," one sees them contracting their brows, holding their breath, stiffening their muscles. If after two minutes they are asked what they have been paying attention to, they cannot reply. They have been concentrating on nothing. They have not been paying attention. They have been contracting their muscles. . . . As [this kind of effort] makes us tired, we have the impression that we have been working. That is an illusion. Tiredness has nothing to do with work. . . . The intelligence only grows and bears fruit in joy.[3]

The implications for the spiritual life are immense. Essential to our growth out of fatalism is a longing for God. More important than any plan or set of techniques is our openness, an openness to every day and each moment.

Real Time and Clock Time

Hope that grows out of trust puts us in a different relationship to the hours and days of our lives. We are constantly tempted to look at time as chronology, as *chronos*, as a series of disconnected incidents and accidents. This is one way we think we can manage time or subdue our tasks. Or a way that we feel the victims of our schedules. For this approach also means that time becomes burdensome. We divide our time into minutes and hours and weeks and let its compartments dominate us.

As still not completely converted people, we immerse ourselves in clock time. Time becomes a means to an end, not moments in which to enjoy God or pay attention to others. And we end up believing that the real thing is always still to come. Time for celebrating or praying or dreaming gets squeezed out. No wonder we get fatigued and deflated! No wonder we sometimes feel helpless or impoverished in our experience of time.

But the gospel speaks of "full" time. What we are seeking is already here. The contemplative Thomas Merton once wrote, "The Bible is concerned with time's fullness, the time for an event to happen, the time for an emotion to be felt, the time for a harvest or for the celebration of a harvest."[4] We begin to see history not as a collection of events interrupting what we "must" get done. We see time in light of faith in the

God of history. We see how the events of this year are not just a series of incidents and accidents, happy or unhappy, but the molding hands of God, who wants us to grow and mature.

Time has to be converted, then, from *chronos*, mere chronological time, to *kairos*, a New Testament Greek word that has to do with opportunity, with moments that seem ripe for their intended purpose. Then, even while life continues to seem harried, while it continues to have hard moments, we say, "Something good is happening amid all this." We get glimpses of how God might be working out his purposes in our days. Time becomes not just something to get through or manipulate or manage, but the arena of God's work with us. Whatever happens—good things or bad, pleasant or problematic—we look and ask, "What might God be doing here?" We see the events of the day as continuing occasions to change the heart. Time points to Another and begins to speak to us of God.

We are part of a very impatient culture, however. We want many things, and we want them quickly. And we feel that we should be able to take away the pains, heal the wounds, fill the holes, and create experiences of great meaningfulness—now. It is not difficult to discover how impatient we are. We have plans and projects we are convinced we want, and then we become irritated when something happens to get in our way.

But a view of time as *kairos* helps us to be patient in believing. If we are patient, in this sense we can look at all events of each day—expected or unexpected—as holding a promise for us. Patience becomes in us the attitude that says that we cannot force life but have to let it grow by its own time and development. Patience lets us see the people we meet, the events of the day, and the unfolding history of our times all part of that slow process of growth.

The other side of our impatience is boredom. When things do not happen the way we planned them, when we do not see that anything great is taking place, when we no longer get distracted by all our plans and projects, we may simply feel bored. Boredom also grows out of our fatalism, for it too reflects the disconnectedness of our experience. A day becomes just another day, a year another year. Everything has already been said, there is nothing new under the sun, and life becomes like a piece of wood drifting in near-motionless water.

It is not always easy to resist impatience and boredom. Jesus told a story of ten virgins who took lamps and went to meet the coming bridegroom. Five were foolish and neglected to bring enough oil (Matt. 25:3). When the bridegroom finally came, their lamps were going out. Like them, when we cannot make the bridegroom come soon, we will sit down in self-complaint. Then our lamps go out. We risk missing the fulfillment of our deepest desires. But the impatient desire to bring into being great things, and the dull boredom we feel when things do not happen our way and we lose interest, shows that we have forgotten that life grows to fullness by waiting, often by suffering.

Shrinking from Prayer

When I taught spirituality classes at Harvard Divinity School, students would sometimes express to me their hopes for a more faithful and prayerful life. "I want to begin again," they might say. Or "I want to be intentional at growing spiritually." "I feel I stand at a turning point."

Some would also admit great hesitancy. "I am afraid of this course," one student wrote me. She knew that opening her life to Christ would entail some discomfort—"Learning to expose the garbage, getting rid of it, and hearing the voice of God in the newly created places." Another worried about the effort required to overcome his deep skepticism. "I want to be a spiritual person," he admitted, "but I resist it."

We will face evil, I told my students. And while we find strength and healing in the Spirit to overcome, I could not promise an easy experience. No one can. We are challenged to offer to God and each other our best, something we do only with disciplined effort. "I would like to work on opening my heart rather than hardening it," one of my students said. He said it well; the gospel awaits fresh discovery in the open places we leave in our hearts.

How do we allow such openness to God's freeing presence to pervade our praying? How often have I heard someone say (and I say it to myself!), "I become so wrapped up in activity that I neglect to pay attention to prayer and the workings of God in my life." A student once likened her relationship with

God to "a kind of fire that provides energy for all the external concerns of my life. . . . I don't want that fire to go out." The answer lies in the twin resources of memory and expectation.

Reading Life Backward

We first look backward to see how our lives' seemingly unrelated events have brought us to where we are. Like the people of Israel who repeatedly reflected on their history and discovered God's guiding hand in the many painful events that led them to Jerusalem, so we pause to discern God's presence in the events that have made us or unmade us. For by not remembering we allow forgotten memories to become independent forces that have a crippling effect on our functioning and relating and praying. George Santayana reminds us that those who forget their past are doomed to repeat it. Forgetting the past is like turning our most intimate teacher against us. It is to guarantee that we cannot find the way to trust and hope.

Sorting through memories means holding painful recollections in a certain way. As Louis Dupré has reminded us, a person neurotically obsessed with the past does not really remember the past, but rather attempts to repeat it; by reliving painful events he or she tries to attain an ending that is different from the one he or she cannot accept. But memory never copies the past; it brings the past into the potentially healing present. It breathes new life into a bygone reality and replaces it with a new context.

Memory also reminds us of the faithfulness of God in the hard places and joyous moments. It lets us see how God has brought good from even the impossible situations. Remembering in this way allows us to live in the present. It does not mean to live in another time but to live in the present with our whole history, with an awareness of the possibilities we might not otherwise think to look for.

Memory, therefore, has much to do with the future. Without memory there is no expectation. Those who have little memory have little to expect. Memory anchors us in the past and then makes us present here and now and opens us up for a new future.

The Forward Look

We will experience the minutes and hours and days of our lives differently when hope takes up residence. In a letter to Jim Forest, who at the time directed the Fellowship of Reconciliation, Thomas Merton wrote, "The real hope is not in something we think we can do, but in God, who is making something good out of it in some way we cannot see."

Hope is not dependent on peace in the land, justice in the world, and success in the business. Hope is willing to leave unanswered questions unanswered and unknown futures unknown. Hope makes you see God's guiding hand not only in the gentle and pleasant moments but also in the shadows of disappointment and darkness.

No one can truly say with certainty where he or she will be ten or twenty years from now. You do not know if you will be free or in captivity, if you will be honored or despised, if you will have many friends or few, if you will be liked or rejected. But when you hold lightly these dreams and fears, you can be open to receive every day as a new day and to live your life as a unique expression of God's love for humankind.

There is an old expression that says, "As long as there is life there is hope." As Christians we also say, "As long as there is hope there is life." Can hope change our lives? Take away our sadness and fatalism? A story helps me answer such questions.

A soldier was captured as a prisoner of war. His captors transported him by train far from his homeland. He felt isolated from country, bereft of family, estranged from anything familiar. His loneliness grew as he continued not to hear anything from home. He could not know that his family was even alive, how his country was faring. He had lost a sense of anything to live for.

But suddenly, unexpectedly, he got a letter. It was smudged, torn at the edges from months of travel. But it said, "We are waiting for you to come home. All is fine here. Don't worry." Everything instantly seemed different. His circumstances had not changed. He did the same difficult labor on the same meager rations, but now he knew someone waited for his release and homecoming. Hope changed his life.

God has written us a letter. The good news of God's revelation in Christ declares to us precisely what we need to hope. Sometimes the words of the Bible do not seem important to us. Or they do not appeal to us. But in those words we hear Christ saying in effect, "I am waiting for you. I am preparing a house for you and there are many rooms in my house." Paul the apostle tells us, "Be transformed by the renewing of your minds" (Rom. 12:2). We hear a promise and an invitation to a life we could not dream of if all we considered were our own resources.

Therein is the hope that gives us new power to live, new strength. We find a way, even in sadness and illness and even death, never to forget how we can hope.

We catch glimmers of this way to live even while we must admit how dimly we see it and imperfectly we live it. "I am holding on to my conviction that I can trust God," I must tell myself sometimes, "because I cannot yet say it fully." I dare to say it even when everything is not perfect, when I know others will criticize my actions, when I fear that my limitations will disappoint many—and myself. But still I trust that the truth will shine through, even when I cannot fully grasp it. Still I believe that God will accomplish what I cannot, in God's own grace and unfathomable might.

The paradox of expectation is that those who believe in tomorrow can better live today; those who expect joy to come out of sadness can discover the beginnings of a new life amid the old; those who look forward to the returning Lord can discover him already in their midst. Just as the love of a mother for her son can grow while she is waiting for his return, just as lovers can rediscover each other after long periods of absence, so our intimate relationship with God can become deeper and more mature while we wait patiently in expectation of his return.

To hope for this growth, to believe even in its possibility, is to say no to every form of fatalism. It is to voice a no to every way we tell ourselves "I know myself—I cannot expect any changes." This no to discouragement and self-despair comes in the context of a yes to life, a yes we say amid even fragile times lived in a world of impatience and violence. For even while we mourn, we do not forget how our life can ultimately join God's larger dance of life and hope.

4

FROM MANIPULATION TO LOVE

If someone asked you if you were compassionate, you might readily say yes. Or at least, "I believe so." But pause to examine the word *compassion* and answering gets more complicated. For the word comes from roots that mean literally to "suffer with"; to show compassion means sharing in the suffering "passion" of another. Compassion understood in this way asks more from us than a mere stirring of pity or a sympathetic word.

To live with compassion means to enter others' dark moments. It is to walk into places of pain, not to flinch or look away when another agonizes. It means to stay where people suffer. Compassion holds us back from quick, eager explanations when tragedy meets someone we know or love.

In some ways you might think such opening ourselves to others' pain would only intensify our own. How many people run to where others are suffering? Who easily hears someone weep or cry out or reveal a quiet sadness? Confronted with poverty or hardship or mourning, we say to ourselves, "Let's go where things feel a little more comfortable." Such is our natural logic.

Even when we do resist the temptation to run and think we listen sympathetically, we may still try to evade or avoid someone's pain. Imagine that someone comes to you and says, "I want to talk to you about my disappointment. I am wondering if I can go on like this much longer." Something in us immediately wants to comfort and console. "It's not as bad as you think," we might be tempted to say. "Look at the bright side; there are good things in this situation."

I recall a time as a priest that I visited a woman who suffered devastating loss after a hurricane and flood swept through her neighborhood. I found her alone, desperately gazing at the damage done to her house. She sat saying to herself, "I am superfluous. I have become meaningless. Since my husband died, I am only a burden for myself, my children, my neighbors. Nobody needs me anymore. There is only one thing left for me to do: to die." Although I knew her typically as talkative and outgoing, now she hardly recognized me.

"You have no reason to be depressed," I said. "Look— you have children who love you and like to visit you. You have charming grandchildren who are happy to have a grandmother to spend time with them. Your son already has plans to come to fix your house. Besides, few people in this neighborhood fared as well as you in the storm."

I did not help her with these words. I made her more depressed, more haunted by guilt, more aware of a pressure to face her world with a smiling face. My words came more as accusation than consolation. "After all," I said in effect, "my arguments for feeling good are better than your arguments for feeling bad." I had not accepted her feelings, but instantly fought her in a subtle competition of arguments. When I left, I went from a woman feeling more sad than before, more burdened because I had not even acknowledged I had heard her. I did not give her permission to feel sad in a sad moment.

In so many encounters we try to look away from the pain. We try to help our friends quickly process grief. We hastily look for ways to bring cheer to a child or ailing aunt. All the while, however, we act less out of genuine "suffering with" and more out of our need to stand back from the discomfort we fear we might feel. We secretly, restlessly want to move from the place where it hurts. Our evasions do not help others, of course, but rather cause them to put up defenses and drive away those who need someone to care.

One reason we react to others this way grows out of our skirting of our own pain. We resist getting near the suffering of another partly out of our unwillingness to suffer ourselves. For another's hardship suggests to us what can also hurt us. Such reminders unsettle. But our hesitation to look squarely at another's suffering, to sit or stand with someone in pain, weighs on conversations an obligation for the other to "act happy." Even worse, our persisting in denying our losses leads to mounting desire to control other people's lives. In his penetrating study, *The Betrayal of the Self,* the psychoanalyst Arno

Gruen shows convincingly how "the actual source of our cruelty and callousness lies in the rejection of our suffering."[1]

For we may fall into the illusion that we own people, that we can use them, that we have a right to manage their feelings. By offering premature advice on how to cope, by rushing to reassure, by prodding with advice, we say much about our own need for easy closure. When we barge in with such consolation, we make hurting souls into objects or projects.

For all the ways this approach seems to insulate us from the hurts and needs of others, it ends up not helping us at all. It barricades us in our own insistence on comfort. Indeed, a possessive approach to relationships creates many of our disappointments; people rarely respond well to our efforts to manage their lives or orchestrate their response to their pains. We find relationships bending or even breaking under the weight of expectations we place on them in our discomfort with another's suffering. We end up even more alone and walled within our disappointments or sadnesses.

Why Others Disappoint

This strain placed on relationships—indeed strains of all kinds—seems to proliferate in a time like ours, when people seem especially interested in friendship, companionship, and community. At the very time when books and articles tout solutions to our relational difficulties, more families than ever fracture and scatter. Fewer young families grow up surrounded by the support of extended family. We live amid great dislocation and anguished loneliness.

And for all the insights of popularized psychology, all the programs on relationships, all the seminars and conferences on healthy relationships, we still often are not happy. And because of our culture's emphasis on psychology and interpersonal relationships, we import a consumer mentality to our intimacies. We expect more of our friends and partners than they can (or want to) give. A fair amount of our suffering comes from our loneliness, a loneliness intensified by our high needs.

The psychiatrist Thomas Hora compares our culture's emphasis on the interpersonal with the interlocking fingers of two hands. The fingers can intertwine only to the point that a stalemate is reached. Then the only movement possible is backward, causing friction and even pain among the tightly woven fingers.

The Christian faith suggests another image: two hands resting together, parallel, in a prayerful gesture, pointing beyond themselves and moving freely in relation to one another. Only in this way can a relationship be truly lasting, because only in this way is mutual love experienced, love that participates in the greater and prior love to which it points. In this way we become persons to one another, in the literal sense of the word's roots: "sounding through" (*per* means "through" and *sonare* suggests the idea of sound). So we "sound through" a love greater than ourselves and one that we can pass along but not clutch. We become people who reveal to each other the divine love that embraces us and keeps us together while offering ample space to move freely.

In the most significant relationships of our lives, God is not an afterthought. We discover one another as living reminders of God's presence. Friendship and marriage and relationships among those in the church community become ways to reveal to one another the original, all-embracing love of God, in which we participate and of which we become human disclosures.

Our Craving for Acceptance

We stumble on this, however, in three significant ways. First, we have difficulty because of our intense need to be justified, a need rooted in our craving to be liked and accepted by the significant (or not-so-significant) people in our lives. Many things we think we do for others are in fact the expressions of our drive to discover our identity in the praise of others. Our needs keep us from acting and loving freely. Writes Thomas Merton,

> He who attempts to act and do things for others or for the world without deepening his own self-understanding, freedom, integrity, and capacity to love, will not have

anything to give to others. He will communicate to them nothing but the contagion of his own obsessions, his aggressiveness, his ego-centered ambitions . . . his doctrinaire prejudices and ideas.[2]

Here lies the center of Merton's critique of our activism, the second way in which we try to manage others or love with conditions. We end up doing things for others for the sake of doing, for the sake of ourselves. This kind of activism gathers merit badges. It is motivated by guilt, by the feeling of being indebted, by the sense of having to earn righteousness or favor—from God or others. Activism ultimately places our own unmet longings at the center of our efforts. It therefore does not help others in a wholesome way.

Thus forms a tragic circle. The more we try to justify ourselves, the more we collide with our inability to do so. The more burdens we take on, the more we burden others with our unmet needs. Is it any wonder that our words do not help, and our presence does not heal? Merton wrote to his friend James Forest:

All the good you will do will come not from you but from the fact that you have allowed yourself, in the obedience of faith, to be used by God's love. Think of this more and gradually you will be free from the need to prove yourself and you can be more open to the power that will work through you without your knowing it.

This happens only with a conviction that God remains active in the world. God acts—always, every moment—in our community and our world. Activism comes from an unbelief that insists that God does not or cannot move and act; it wants to replace God's supposed slowness or inaction with our activity. But we should intend that what we do to help and serve and minister does not create in the absence of God, but respond to what God is already bringing into being.

Prayer, which puts us in contact with this God regularly, makes others into something more than characters to be criticized, judged, and misjudged. It makes them into more than objects of pity or "projects" in need of our wonderful gifts. It rather helps us see them as persons to be received—loved with a love implanted in us and already at work in the world.

This also helps us with the third stumbling block to truly loving others: our competitiveness. And how competitive we are! We want to make our mark in life; we want to be different, special. On very subtle levels we compete without wanting to, often without realizing it. We compare ourselves to others and worry about what others think of us even when we are serving others. We wonder if we serve better than someone else. We import a drive to achieve into our works of mercy.

We do this so much that we even sometimes form our identities in comparison to others; we certainly never completely admit the possibility of giving up our sense of difference, of entering where others are weak, of sharing with another's pain. We have too much of ourselves and our ambitions to defend to easily allow that.

Is Compassion Possible?

We discover, then, that for all our good intentions, compassion does not form the true basis of our lives. Compassion does not come as our spontaneous response but goes against the grain. We might wonder if it is humanly possible!

Such a view has a healthy consequence. Compassion in its fullest sense can be attributed only to God. It is the central message of the gospel that God, who in no way is in competition with us, is the One who can be truly compassionate. It is because Jesus was not dependent on people, but only on God, that he could be so close to people, so concerned, so confronting, so healing, so caring. He related to people for their own sake, not his own. To say it in more psychological terms, he paid attention without intention. His question was not "How can I receive satisfaction?" but "How can I respond to your real need?" This is possible only when there is a deeper satisfaction, a deeper intimacy from whence attention can be paid. Your love for others can be unconditional, without a condition that your needs are gratified, when you have the experience of being loved.

Think about the people who have most influenced you. When I remember them, I am always surprised to discover that these are people who did not try to influence me, who did not need my response. Instead they radiated a certain inner freedom. They made me aware that they were in touch with more than themselves. They pointed to a reality greater than themselves from which and in whom their freedom grew. This centeredness, this inner freedom, this spiritual independence had a mysterious contagiousness.

Real ministry starts taking place when we bring others in touch with more than we ourselves are—the center of being, the reality of the unseen—the Father who is the source of life and healing.

Twin Agents of Good

With that in mind, how do we move to a place of deep and transforming love? How can experiencing more fully the joys and pains of other people lead us from our dungeon of self and bring us greater joy? How can it bring healing to our fractured relationships? How can God's compassion become ours? We can love only because we have first been loved. In prayer Jesus finds a lonely place where this first love is realized. We can serve people only when we do not make our total sense of self dependent on their response.

This approach can take root in us with two disciplines. Solitude, to begin, does not mean so much withdrawing in silence out of antisocial sentiments. Solitude means that our aloneness sometimes does not come as a sad fact needing healing but rather offers a place where God comes to bring communion. In fact, solitude has rich roots and connotations significantly different from two other words often associated with it: *Aloneness* generally means being by oneself in a neutral way. *Loneliness* more suggests the pain of desolation or another's absence. But *solitude* carries notes of joy and possibility. For solitude, for the Christian, means not just to wander off to woods or desert or mountaintop for private withdrawal. It means daring to stand in God's presence. Not to guard time simply to be alone, but alone in God's company.

What do you do when alone with God? Many of us think, talk, or ask. But when alone with God how vital also to listen! Solitude is the place where you can hear the voice that calls you the beloved, that leads you on to the next page of the adventure, that says, as God said to Jesus early in the Gospels, "This is my son, the Beloved, with whom I am well pleased" (Matt. 3:17).

How vitally that word *beloved* can resound across our lives! Can you hear it? Everyone hears voices that seem to speak for God: "Prove yourself. Do something that makes you significant and then I will show up in love." Or we hear, "Do something relevant; be sure that people speak well of you. Be sure you gather money and property and influence; then I will love you." In our insecurity we try very hard to respond to such voices. And then we stay busy proving to others that we deserve some attention, that we are good people worth praise, that we merit affection or attention.

We push ourselves to wield influence or make a mark. Often we call that "vocation," but Jesus calls it "temptation." He has no patience with the one who insists that he jump from the temple to show his power or turn stones into bread to prove his ministry credentials. He has heard God speak of his belovedness as God's Son. That forms the basis of what he does and knows himself called to do. He will not be distracted by merely doing superficial good. He bears the very presence of God.

It is hard for us to hear the voice that proclaims that we are loved in Christ, not for our reputation or impressive actions, but because God has loved us with an everlasting love. "I don't hear anything," some say. We are too prone, too conditioned to listen for all the other voices that insist on "success" or "results." I hear only the voices that urge me to go here or do that or get done this mandate, we sometimes think. But then we also long for that other voice.

I do not suggest by this that you or I should not see fruit from our ministries, not own property, or not enjoy any possessions. I am not saying we should not want to find affection and love from others. I am saying, however, that our identity can find its basis only in God's word to us that we are beloved, not on the world's fickle promises. In Christ we live as God's beloved before we were born and after we have died; all the circumstances in between will not negate that.

L'Arche communities began as a network of communities like Daybreak. The first of the communities began not as a big organization, but when someone with a heart for two people with significant disabilities invited them to live together and form a community of faith and service and worship. It began with someone saying, "Take two poor people and start living with them."

It was not hard to find two men with Down syndrome, two poor people with no father or mother or other family, no visitors or friends. That first community began with a rented house and an invitation that said, "Let's create a family atmosphere here." They called it The Ark, after Noah's ark in the Bible (*L'Arche* in French). And out of those simple beginnings, hatched in solitary listening, grew a network of 156 global communities with thousands of members, those with intellectual disabilities and their assistants, in little homes across the world.[3]

Talk of solitude has immense applications for how we live with our wounds and live with others as wounded people. For we spend much time figuring out who hurt us and where our scars show. We have gotten wounded along the way by the very people who love us—our parents, our children, our colleagues, our friends and spouses. Because no one can meet our deepest needs for love, so must we learn, in our solitude, to forgive.

Constantly we find this a challenge. Before I go to breakfast in the morning, I have twenty thoughts of people who should, I think, be just a little different from what they are: if they would just shape up, or not always arrive late; if they would not act so brusquely. . . . We must constantly learn to offer compassion in such situations because we have a heart that desires things that are complete, and we live—always—in situations that can seem only incomplete. We walk with (or bump into) people who always live and love imperfectly.

Still, in the midst of people who have loved us well or not so well, God's love reaches to us. If we can make it out above the static and disruptions of noisy lives, we realize it came before anyone touched us or harmed us. This love will always exist, even after we die. Solitude, where we absent ourselves from the myriad voices that tell us otherwise, helps us hear again that voice of love.

If you believe that you are the beloved, you can offer forgiveness, even when it cannot be received. For still you say, "I set you free and I am willing to forgive you even when you cannot forgive me, because I claim my belovedness." And you can move on, saying, "I can ask your forgiveness even though you cannot give it to me yet, and perhaps ever."

Solitude does not present itself easily to us, of course. Much conspires against it in ringing phones and high-tech connections that leave us never far from someone's demand for our time and attention. Have you ever tried simply to sit in a chair for an hour—no television, phone, or chatty conversation? Even if you manage to seclude yourself amid quiet relief from a noisy society, inner voices can rise up to noisily distract you.

Why else would we speak of solitude as a discipline? It asks of us a bit of attention. This is especially because, in our loneliness, we rarely seem completely to ignore rejection or uselessness. We want to get going to confirm to our insecure selves that we are truly there. To be alone with God in silence asks us not to attend to these incessant influences. We resolve to wait in the quiet of time with God for communion and for insight deeper than we could manufacture.

To solitude we add the twin discipline of silence. We participate in the life of the Spirit through all we hear and say—and what we determine not to hear and say. For our listening in silence can manifest the Spirit within and among us, just as surely as our words of salvation and our acts of healing.

Of course, silence can be fearsome. Many people are silenced and cowed by fear. Silence can be paralyzing, oppressive. Nothing new can be born out of such silence. And words not born of silent listening can afflict and hurt. Many people are "wordy" and use speech to oppress and manipulate. Talking becomes opportunistic. Such words do not heal or aid communion. They do not foster the rich silence of communion but crowd our lives with clutter.

Liberation in this context means restoring the intimate relationship between silence and the word, so that both can bear fruit. We find the appropriate times to speak, to stretch out our hands, to inspire with our words. But we just as surely learn when our silence ministers most deeply. This happens when God sends his Spirit. After all, we experience God through both silence and words. Jesus, we learn from the Gospels, "went out to a deserted place, and there he prayed" (Mark 1:35). And yet he also spoke the words given to him (John 14:10). Both found a place, but in silence he learned the appropriate word.

When Solitude Meets Solitude

And here we gain clues about what it means to live in a community as a person of faith and compassion, one who can genuinely help the hurting and bring love to others' suffering. For community is more than people living together; it is also solitude greeting solitude. Healing encounters and deep communion with others come about from persons who have experienced at least a taste of love offering love to another, without manipulation or subtle games.

Loneliness greeting loneliness, need smashing into need, of course, looks different. Such encounters entangle people in complex and difficult situations. No wonder we have trouble getting along as human persons! I am not so sure but that when I go to care for another person a deep part of me longs to say, "Please love me. Without you I cannot live." And before you know it, I come not to hold in love but to grab in the intensity of neediness.

We become violent precisely because we expect more from each other than we can give. When we look for divine solutions in others, we make others into gods and ourselves into demons. Our hands no longer caress but instead grasp. Our lips no longer kiss or form kind words but bite. Our eyes no longer look expectantly but suspiciously. Our ears do not hear so much as overhear. Every time we think that another person or group of people is finally going to come and take away our fear and anxiety, we will find ourselves so frustrated that, instead of becoming gentle, we will become violent.

Community, then, cannot grow out of loneliness, but comes when the person who begins to recognize his or her belovedness greets the belovedness of the other. The God alive in me greets the God resident in you. When people can cease having to be for us everything, we can accept the fact they may still have a gift for us. They are partial reflections of the great love of God, but reflections nevertheless. We see that gift precisely and only once we give up requiring that person to be everything, to be God. We see him or her as a limited expression of an unlimited love.

To live and serve and worship with others thereby brings us to a place where we come together and remind each other by our mutual interdependence that we are not God, that we cannot meet our own needs, and that we cannot completely fulfill each other's needs. There is something wonderfully humbling and freeing about this. For we find a place where people give one another grace. That we are not God does not mean that we cannot mediate (if in a limited way) the unlimited love of God. Community is the place of joy and celebration where we are willing to say, "Yes, we have begun to overcome in Christ."

Such is the victory of the cross. Love is stronger than death, and the community is the place where we continue to let the world know there is something to rejoice about in this new life together, something to be ecstatic about—that is, to move out of the static place of death and declare that human beings need not be afraid. Gratitude springs from an insight, a recognition that something good has come from another person, that it is freely given to me, and meant as a favor. And at the moment this recognition dawns on me, gratitude spontaneously arises in my heart. I need no longer always manage and muster support for my "cause."

Beyond Manipulation

Living with others can also break us out of our narrow points of view. When we relate to life (and others) as properties to be possessed or controlled or conquered, we cannot rightly see. Grab a flower and it cannot long reveal its beauty to you; it will wither. If you apply pressure to a friend's weak spot to subdue, he or she cannot become your friend. Relate to people as a conqueror and they will hide their real nature from you. Violence is the brother and distrust the sister of this way of life. What you relate to in a manipulative way does not reveal itself to you. It closes itself; it hides its real nature; it becomes opaque.

As long as we relate to one another this way, persons cannot be more than just characters to be defined, labeled, categorized, manipulated. But prayer helps us here. When in prayer we see all of life as a gift, then people become the greatest gift. They are no longer chess pieces to move around or allies in our schemes and ambitions, but persons with whom to form community, from whom to learn. In prayer we discover that people are more than their character, and when we become persons to each other, we "sound through" a peace greater than we ourselves can make and a love deeper and wider than we ourselves can contain.

When we become persons, we become transparent to each other, and light can shine through us, God can speak through us. When we become persons who transcend the limitations of our individual characters, the God who is love can reveal himself in our midst and bind us into a community. We become transparent. Others lose their opaqueness and reveal to us the loving face of our Lord.

Our society makes it difficult to see people as transparent because we relate to others quite often as characters in a play—different, interesting characters whom we can use for different purposes. "He is good in this," we say. "She is good at that." We want to use people. Sometimes, of course, we must relate to people in their appropriate roles. We expect teachers to teach, telephone operators to help us find numbers. But still we remember also that a person is more than his or her role. If you see in me more than my function or job, then I can slowly communicate to you on a deeper level. I can become a person to you.

And by truly meeting another we come into contact with a great beauty and sense of awe. We are often shining through each other the realities that we ourselves do not see, that we do not even fully understand. A prayerful life, then, is one in which we convert the world from darkness, people from mere roles to persons.

The End of Enemies

The message of the gospel brims with compassion, with a love that willingly "suffers with," even with those we do not naturally like. Jesus reveals to us through his words and actions, but most of all through his life and death, that God is love, even toward the unlovely and unlovable. Jesus calls us to make this divine love the basis of our lives. "This is my commandment," said Jesus, "that you love one another as I have loved you" (John 15:12).

The full implications of this call to love are hard to grasp. The kind of love Jesus calls us to includes the enemy, not just the friendly neighbor. Such love may in many ways run counter to our desires, needs, or expectations. Our understanding of love is so strongly influenced by ideas from interpersonal human relationships—personal attraction, mutual compatibility, sexual desires, cultural understandings of sensitivity—that we have trouble realizing that the love of God goes far beyond these.

During the course of Christian history, love of enemies has been often seen as the core of sanctity. Staretz Silouan, a twentieth-century Greek Orthodox monk, wrote, "If you pray for your enemies, peace will come to you. And when you love your enemies, take for certain that great divine grace dwells in you."[4]

The test of love is our forgiveness of enemies; just as Jesus forgave (Luke 23:34), so are we to. Just as Stephen, the first Christian martyr, followed his Lord when being stoned, he prayed, "Lord, do not hold this sin against them" (Acts 7:60). This is not easy, of course, largely because of the ways we continue to crave attention, affection, influence, power, even after hearing God's word that we are his beloved. These needs are born from our wounds and never seem to be satisfied. When we try to find an explanation for these wounds, we discover how they have been inflicted on us by people who are needy people themselves. Through the generations there seems to run a chain of wounds and needs. And when we try to avoid inflicting wounds ourselves, we discover that even with our best intentions we cannot avoid encountering people who feel rejected, misunderstood, or hurt by us.

Thus there seems to be a long chain of interlocking

wounds and needs that stretch back into the long past and forward into our future. This picture drives us to turn love into a kind of mechanical exchange: "I will love you if you love me; I will give to you if you give to me; I will lend to you if you give me the same amount." As long as we continue to search for our deepest sense of who we are among other people, we will end up dividing the world into people who are for us and people who are against us, people who accept us and people who reject us—friends and enemies.

The gospel liberates us from the chain of wounds and needs by revealing to us a compassion that can do more than react out of the needs that grow from our wounds. It does so by bringing us into contact with an acceptance that precedes any human acceptance or rejection. And this original love is all-embracing; it holds the power to love enemies as well as friends, the power to allow us to love in that way. This is the love that makes us be sons and daughters of the "Most High," who "is kind to the ungrateful and the wicked" (Luke 6:35). "He makes his sun rise on the evil and on the good, and sends rain on the righteous and on the unrighteous" (Matt. 5:45).

When our love grows from God's love, we no longer divide people into those who deserve it and those who don't. It is this love that allows us to see the enemy as someone loved with the same love with which we are loved. We need no longer define ourselves over and against the other. To love as Christ loved means a participation in the divine love that does not know a distinction between friend and enemy.

Martin Luther King Jr. wrote, "An overflowing love which seeks nothing in return, *agape*, is the love of God operating in the human heart. At this level, we love people not because we like them nor because they possess some type of divine spark; we love all human beings because God loves them."[5]

We remember that in one sense enemies are enemies only by our insistence on excluding them in our hearts from the love of God. "Be merciful, just as your Father is merciful," Jesus tells us. "Do not judge, and you will not be judged; do not condemn, and you will not be condemned. Forgive, and you will be forgiven" (Luke 6:36–37).

And here we learn yet another lesson: how God's divine love reduces us to humility, a kind of inner poverty. "Blessed are the poor," Jesus said in the Sermon on the Mount. Note that he did not say, "Blessed are those who care for the poor" (though he certainly commended elsewhere those who helped the "least" and the needy). In one sense, everyone in the body of Christ is poor. But when we come together in mutual poverty, in shared vulnerability, we offer to and receive from one another.

In our poverty hides great blessing, for God decided to reveal God's glory in vulnerability and brokenness, not in commanding presence or manipulative authority. That is what the cross teaches us anew. When John the Evangelist beheld the broken Christ of the crucifixion, he saw blood and water coming from Christ's side (John 19:34). And we too perceive a gift flowing from the broken body that gave life, that will give new life to our communities and our relationships. We will suffer, and suffer with one another, but in doing so we will uncover nothing less than the presence of a God whose consolation keeps us going.

Pain suffered alone feels very different from pain suffered alongside another. Even when the pain stays, we know how great the difference if another draws close, if another shares with us in it. This kind of comfort comes most fully and powerfully visible in the incarnation, wherein God comes into our midst—into our lives—to remind us, "I am with you at all times and in all places." In Christ God draws near us amid our sufferings—the pain of infants or adolescents, the hurts of young adults or the aged, the griefs of the unemployed and the suddenly single person. There is no human suffering that has not in some way been part of God's experience. That is the great and wonderful mystery of God becoming flesh to live among us. God becomes a part of our mourning and invites us to learn to dance—not alone, but with others, sharing in God's own compassion, as we both give it and receive it.

5

FROM A FEARFUL DEATH
TO A JOYOUS LIFE

Two times I came very close to dying. In the first brush with death, a van struck me while I walked along a trafficked suburban road. The collision knocked me unconscious, and I awoke in a hospital, surrounded by concerned nurses and doctors.

Not many years later, I landed in the hospital again, this time with a dangerous infection. Exhaustion from a relentless schedule had left me in a poor position to fight the disease. I could have died then as well.

At these times death no longer hovered on the outskirts of my consciousness. As I recovered from each brush with death, I realized how few people are ready to die. Most people I know are not preparing themselves unless circumstances compel them. How rarely do we look at death, even when close to it! We routinely forget how God makes our lives part of a larger life that stretches far beyond the horizons of birth and death.

A friend of mine is dying. How I wish that he could be healed! But I also know that the final healing for him, for all of us, means something more than a release from physical ailments or a deteriorating body. Our life span, whether thirty years or ninety, gives us opportunities to say yes to a hidden gift from God, to a reality that, while difficult, provides a place for divine encounter and deep growth. To find healing means to belong completely to God, to be born into a life and love that is lasting. It has to do more with seeking first God's kingdom and finding the deepest longings of our hearts fulfilled than the condition of our bodies.

Facing death, thought of this way, need not come as a maudlin exercise. Instead it proves a way to celebrate our life as God's beloved sons and daughters so that we live our last days, be they few or many, as days of constant opening to what is to come. The God who made us and who called us "beloved" before we were born lives with us and in us. Nothing can separate us from that love of God in Christ, even amid the reality, which much in us prefers to ignore or avoid, of death. For living with joy through both life and death requires that we learn to discern the voice of divine love in every eventuality. How rarely do I walk through my daily existence with that eternal perspective! But such discoveries have a great deal to do not only with our final end but our daily life.

Trapped in Humanness

This daily life, however, reminds us constantly of our inner brokenness and outer hardship. Struggles with family, pressures at work, conflicts with friends leave us feeling small and insignificant. Illness or chronic pain makes us realize our physical vulnerability. We frequently feel guilty or ashamed over ways we make wrong choices or hurt others. Sometimes we feel trapped in our humanness. We experience keenly how things fall short of our expectations.

We try in many ways to free ourselves from our entrapment. We think more money will rescue us, perhaps, or another job, another spouse, a better house, a new diet or exercise program, or a better self-understanding. All of these approaches strive for change from below. Like sheep caught in a thorny bush, the harder we struggle to get out the more entangled we become.

It is true that we may need to work to change our circumstances at times; we may rightly find ourselves occasionally restless. After all, our hearts do not rest content with a little bit of life, a taste of love. We desire all of life and love because God made our hearts and gave us something of his boundless heart. We want to be more than we are.

But the changes we propose, our resolutions and new programs and self-help schemes, will not ultimately free us because we continue to move within the constraints of mortality. We all eventually die. We cannot escape our earthly limits. We must live knowing that we someday will die.

This can discourage us, of course. It leads some to despair. But we can also discern in the very disappointments life gives us chances to reflect hopefully on our mortality. Birth, going to school, attending college, marrying, getting a first job, and retiring all provide us with opportunities to let go of what we find familiar. They usher into our lives "small deaths." They remind us that fear and love are born at the same time. Both are never entirely separated in our existence. But as we come into contact with these little deaths, we meet life. They allow us to learn to let go. They prepare us to discover a life different from what we have known before.

Life is a school in which we are trained to depart. That is what mortification really means: training to die, to cut away the enslaving ties with the past. So that what we call death is not a surprise anymore, but the last of many gateways that lead to the full human person.

The End Out of Sight

Why do we not prepare ourselves for death when we live so close to it? I observe much death avoidance in our culture. We try to cover it with cosmetics and platitudes. We cannot even imagine good coming from difficulty and mortality. When someone suffers, we want to stay away; when someone dies, we want not to face fully his or her death. We say, "He passed away," or "She left us." While one certainty is that each person will die, we deny death as if it is the most unreal thing. The way we bury people in our society strikes me as a sophisticated way of denying death's reality. We hide it from view. When people we love die, we surround them with flowers and cry for them in lavishly, soothingly decorated rooms. We do not see dead people often and if we do, we tend to keep our children away.

A friend of mine had a little bird in a cage that he found dead one morning. He so feared for his small son to see the lifeless bird that he ran to the store to buy a new one to put in the cage before his son discovered what had happened. He did not want to have to tell his son that we do not live forever. No matter that the bird my friend so strove to replace was not the same bird, nor could it be. He betrayed a conviction born of fear: that we must avoid death at all costs, even if it means not valuing the uniqueness of each life.

In our relationships with one another, sometimes we act as though we prefer the illusion that we live immortally. We forget that we will see each other only for a relatively short time. That you or I might not be here tomorrow, next week, next year. And so we avoid death rather than value life for all its preciousness.

Those who do not avoid death may romanticize it. Our culture's denial of death appears along with an ironic companion: a fascination with death. We see this allure in the entertainment world, with its dark images of violence, with song lyrics that exalt the macabre. We see it on the world stage, where billions of dollars go toward military budgets and instruments of warfare, and people glorify combat. We substitute the legitimate grief of death and dying in favor of an unrealistic, even sentimentalized view.

Jesus would instead call us to a simple, clear-eyed look at death. Consider how Jesus raised Lazarus from the dead in John's Gospel. Perhaps like some of the onlookers in the story, we want only the miracle of someone raised from the dead. We see the promise of the cure but do not as easily see the care, the participation in suffering, the sharing of the pain. What we do not want to see are the tears and the deep sorrow that drove Jesus to pray to his Father.

Jesus, however, does not want us to avoid such a confrontation. Is it any accident that he came to the scene of the mourning and grieving well after Lazarus's death? He had heard days before that Lazarus had fallen ill. Still, he waited. Did he perhaps want no one to doubt that Lazarus was truly dead? When Jesus ordered the tomb opened, Martha, the sister of the dead man, protested, "Already there is a stench because he has been dead four days" (John 11:39). But Jesus' call to life came forth from his tears and from the sigh arising from the depth of his heart.

Our death can become a sign of glory. Jesus showed how precious our life really is: he cried, he mourned. And out of that mourning new life was born. It is through death that we deeply touch life. As a small boy I wanted to be an exception. I wanted no death, no suffering. But now I realize that God wants me to partake in the experience of death. As I do he will strengthen my hope in the midst of it.

Lessons in Loss

It is not just death that unsettles us, of course. It is the process of dying also. The slow deterioration of body and mind, the pain of a spreading cancer, the prospect of burdening friends, an inability to control our movements, a tendency to forget recent events or the names of family members, the suspicion that loved ones tell us only half the truth to "protect us"—all this understandably frightens us. No wonder we sometimes say, "I hope it won't take long. I hope I die of an unexpected heart attack and not a prolonged disease." We would manage and orchestrate even our final exit.

But no matter when or how we die, we inevitably give up an insistence on controlling the details. What is death? I do not know, and you do not know. We find ourselves reduced to admitting that death comes in ways highly unique and individualized. Who can predict? But one thing rings certain: in death we take a jump, we let loose, surrender, give up the safe place we know as comfortable—whether we readily do so or not. Death sometimes strikes us as dry as the desert of Sinai and as lonesome as the cross. Consider some of our forebears in faith: Moses could not know every twist ahead on the road on which he led the people out of Egypt. Jesus jumped into incredible darkness, crying from the cross, "My God, my God, why have you forsaken me?" (Matt. 27:46). Still he did not throw himself down from the cross; still he carried out his Father's will to redeem the world.

We don't know what is beyond our life. We cannot forecast anything about the future for certain; any attempt of our fantasy to fill the emptiness with wish-fulfilling concreteness is more a sign of weak faith than of strong hope. Faith asks us to jump, to surrender and believe that somewhere, somehow, Someone will catch us and bring us home.

Because of such convictions, we can face dying with more than dread or avoidance. We can learn to live well all the more because we do not insist on ignoring what we cannot predict. Learning how to die has something to do with living each day in full awareness that we are children of God, whose love is stronger than death. And as we learn to do so, we find ourselves, in small ways at first, beginning not to cling to what we have, not in panic trying to reserve the safe place we can clamp on to in the here and now. We admit we don't know what the next day will hold, what our loved ones will say or do next, what God may be about in the year ahead. But this does not dispirit us because we also remind ourselves that we never will find out if we do not open our choices to the risk.

Every time that we are able to enjoy the present and still know that tomorrow will hold at least some difficult moments, some uncertainties, some reminders of our mortality, we can learn to stretch out our arms to the Other we trust, to the great Another. We leave the safe ground and start exploring a new field. We break through the walls of our inborn conservatism, ensconced in our need to cling to what we have and know and hoard. And then we experience a liberation through surrender; we learn to make our anxiety hope and our death an exodus.

Remember what Jesus talked about with Moses and Elijah on the moment of his glorification, his transfiguration?

[Jesus] was transfigured before [Peter and James and John], and his clothes became dazzling white, such as no one on earth could bleach them. And there appeared to them Elijah with Moses, who were talking with Jesus. Then Peter said to Jesus, "Rabbi, it is good for us to be here; let us make three dwellings, one for you, one for Moses, and one for Elijah." He did not know what to say, for they were terrified. Then a cloud overshadowed them, and from the cloud there came a voice, "This is my Son, the Beloved; listen to him!" Suddenly when they looked around, they saw no one with them any more, but only Jesus.

As they were coming down the mountain, he ordered them to tell no one about what they had seen, until after the Son of Man had risen from the dead. So they kept the matter to themselves, questioning what this rising from the dead could mean. Then they asked him, "Why do the scribes say that Elijah must come first?" He said to them, "Elijah is indeed coming first to restore all things. How then is it written about the Son of Man, that he is to go through many sufferings and be treated with contempt?"

(MARK 9:2–12)

Here, even in this shining moment of bright ecstasy, Jesus speaks of his suffering and death. Jesus spoke with the leader of the exodus from Egypt to the promised land about his new and final exodus through death to resurrection, an exodus for all who would follow him. It would have to take him on a trip through darkness to light, through suffering to redemption, through pain to healing, but God would carry him and bring out of his death, life.

If death does not become a part of our present it never will be our exodus to the future. As we break through our need to cling to what we have, what we know, what we possess, we can be liberated by trustful surrender to God. Then our anxiety will not cripple us, but point us forward in joy, point us even to what we cannot predict or fully see, even our own death. Indeed, the New Testament paints a portrait of an eternal life that begins now: "See what love the Father has given us, that we should be called children of God; and that is what we are. . . . Beloved, we are God's children now; what we will be has not yet been revealed. What we do know is this:

when he is revealed, we will be like him, for we will see him as he is" (1 John 3:1–2).

The Unshakable Promise

The certainty of such realities does not suggest that our growing convictions will not be tested. In the presence of death we sometimes feel forsaken. The New Testament calls death the "last enemy" for a reason (1 Cor. 15:26). Jesus' encounter with it on the cross came at a great cost. He himself turned to the anguished words of Psalm 22 to voice the dereliction death can sometimes mean: "My God, my God, why have you forsaken me?" (Ps. 22:1)

Jesus' cry in his hour of death reminds us how we can pray this psalm, for all its poignancy, believing that God will live up to God's promises and be with us even in the midst of our anguish. For note that the psalmist, for all his sense of forsaken abandonment, calls upon God. Absence and presence touch one another. Out of his utter pain and forsakenness comes an intimate prayer: "My God, my God." The God the psalmist fears has turned his gaze away is still a God he can address. And will address. The One who seems far from our plea is the One to whom we still turn.

Indeed, the psalmist feels God's hand while cringing before the threatening claws of dogs. He waits for God's word from the mouth of the lion, comes to know God's tender care bending over him through the horns of an oxen. While filled with illness and suffering injustice, he feels the hand of the Almighty. He hears the invitation to be with God while surrounded by aggressors. "In you our ancestors trusted," he remembers; "they trusted, and you delivered them" (Ps. 22:4).

Think not only of this psalmist, not only of Jesus on the cross, praying for those who would kill him, but also Jews praying for their torturers in concentration camps. Think of those who in wrenching extremity in Sudan or South America remember to call on God. For the journey of Christ did not end on the cross. On the road to Emmaus we see the picture changed from despair to hope. In all the times that Jesus appeared to his disciples, victorious over death, we see a picture of another way, a certainty that allows us not to despair either. That allows us to hope that the journey from life to death leads finally from death to life.

Saying Goodbye

"It is to your advantage that I go away," Jesus told his fear-struck, still-confused disciples when they looked ahead together to his death (John 16:7). The subject of this day's teaching from him is departure. He must speak of leaving behind, going away, saying goodbye, wishing farewell. Hearing such words we may first feel sadness. And if you have been at places where ships, planes, and trains leave for far destinations, you have seen many tears when close ties were broken, and people moved away from each other.

But Jesus' farewell shows a different mood. He announces his painful departure as a thing of promise. "It is to your advantage that I go away," he said, "for if I do not go away, the Advocate will not come to you; but if I go, I will send him to you" (John 16:7). In these words, departing has lost its fatality. They will no longer see Jesus but will experience the even more constant presence of the Holy Spirit, whom Jesus will send. Pain and joy, anxiety and freedom, losing a friend and gaining a friend do not fight as opposites anymore, but come together in this deeper emotion of hope that often lies beyond articulation. All because even in the loss of what is dearest, God comes alongside us and becomes our closest companion.

We must face not only our own deaths, then, but willingly allow for the deaths of those we know and love and live with. Departing comes as a condition of life, a condition for Christian growth. Jesus' farewell brings a quiet invitation to understand our life as a constant departure from the familiar to the eternal, from what we enjoy in temporary ways to what we will one day enjoy forever. And we will experience the departure of others. They too partake of this world's inevitable transitions.

We are helped in this letting go of those dear to us through remembering for them and what we remember for ourselves. When we leave the safe body of our mother, we are ready to breathe on our own and to start on the road to selfhood. When we depart from the close center of the family where we are the center of attention, and go to school, we have the chance to test our potentialities and develop new friendships. When we leave home to attend college, we receive the freedom to reevaluate the many things given to us and integrate what we consider as meaningful. When we leave our parents to marry or enter religious life, we can experience the challenge to build our own home and to give life to others. And when we retire from our work, we may have the long-delayed possibility to come to terms with some of the basic dimensions of life.

If life, then, is a constant departure, a constant dying away from the past, to reach more independence, more freedom, and more truth, if our final departure gives us the final independence, freedom, and truth for which we have been groping throughout our entire lives, why could it not be for those we love?

If this is true, death is no longer the cruel destiny of man that ruins all efforts, turns every attempt to live into ridicule, and crushes all creativity into meaningless crumbs—it is a signal to deeper understanding. And in the light of Christ's departure, we can say that we can love not in spite of death, but because of it. Let me tell you a fairy tale.

Once upon a time there was a young man who was living in a big city. Every evening he went to the same restaurant and ate at the same table. He felt very alone. But one day he saw that there was a beautiful rose on his table and a feeling of warmth came into his heart. And he came back day after day and looked at the rose during his meals. Sometimes he was sad, sometimes happy, sometimes indifferent, sometimes angry. But although his moods were different, he noticed that the rose was always the same. He did not understand.

And then, very carefully, he touched the rose—a thing he never dared to do before. But when he felt the hard edges of the leaves, he suddenly realized that the rose did not live. It was a plastic rose. And the young man stood up in anger, pulled the rose out of the dry vase, and crushed it between his fingers. Then he cried and felt more alone than ever before.

We are not made to love immortal things. Only what is irreplaceable, unique, and mortal can touch our deepest human sensitivities and be a source of hope and consolation. God only became lovable when he became mortal. He became our Savior because his mortality was not fatal but the way to hope.

We have seen many departing from us. Thousands are leaving: great leaders, dear friends, and many others unknown but part of our lives. We loved them because they could not be replaced, because they were human. Perhaps we may start seeing through Christ's farewell that even these days can be days of hope, making free the way for the Spirit to come, to open the closed doors of our fears and lead us to the full freedom and the full truth.

And to gratitude. The main character and narrator of the

novel *My Name Is Asher Lev* discovered something of this. He longed to draw and paint as an artist from his youngest days.

> And I drew, too, the way my father once looked at a bird lying on its side against the curb near our house. It was Shabbos [Sabbath] and we were on our way back from the synagogue.
>
> "Is it dead, Papa?" I was six and could not bring myself to look at it.
>
> "Yes," I heard him say in a sad and distant way.
>
> "Why did it die?"
>
> "Everything that lives must die."
>
> "Everything?"
>
> "Yes."
>
> "You, too, Papa? And Mama?"
>
> "Yes."
>
> "And me?"
>
> "Yes," he said. Then he added . . . , "But may it be only after you live a long and good life, my Asher."
>
> I couldn't grasp it. I forced myself to look at the bird. Everything alive would one day be as still as that bird?
>
> "Why?" I asked.
>
> "That's the way the Ribbono Shel Olom made His world, Asher."
>
> "Why?"
>
> "So life would be precious, Asher. Something that is yours forever is never precious."[1]

The Final Healing?

I have a friend who said to me on his deathbed, "The final healing will be that I can hear the voice of love, experience true freedom, and have the deepest desire of my heart fulfilled." If we hold more lightly our lives and give ourselves away to God, we will live closer to God, we will find ourselves ever more grateful, but not likely more popular and successful. Dying is about giving yourself away, trusting yourself to God. What we receive has more of the intangible about it than the worldly prosperous. It may look simple indeed.

I was preparing to celebrate Communion during one of our chapel services at the L'Arche community. A woman, hardly able to speak because of disability, came up to me and said, "Could you give me a blessing?"

"Sure!" I replied, and I prepared to offer a formal prayer, lifting my hand and arm robed with a long, flowing sleeve.

"No," she interrupted, "I mean a real blessing."

She wanted a hug! She wanted me to put my whole self into it. Of course I obliged, and then told her, "You are the beloved of God. And you are very unique." That satisfied her.

Immediately another member of our community said, "I want that too." Soon there were others. A twenty-five-year-old man, an assistant who had come to live and serve in our community after college, came up. "Evan," I said, "I'm so happy you're here." I put my arms around him and said, "My holding you is God holding you and saying, 'You are the beloved son.'

Trust that and live your life in that." His whole body relaxed. It was as though no one had ever told him this. But now he was ready to hear it.

It was the poor, the handicapped people among us, who were the first to teach us to ask for a blessing. Those who suffered most led the way, gave us a profound lesson from amid their own need. Those who might well die at a younger age than many of us, because of their disabilities, had discovered the deep longing at the heart of every life. They had found an unquenchable hope.

None of us ultimately avoids the reality of death, for all our denial; none of us can undo many of the "givens" we inherit at birth. Someone, not some new thing, has to free us, rescue us. Someone from above. Jesus would say to us, "I want to give you my love, my heart, my breath, the Spirit. I want to lift you into my own circle of love. Not after you are dead, but now, in this life, so that you feel forgiven, loved, free."

We still ache in grief when death visits those we love or flinch when it approaches us, of course. We will suffer in many ways. But our pangs will be more like labor pains that bring new life. That bring into our world a new life. Facing death allows us to experience that life in a way our denial never can permit. Inviting God into our grief will mean we never walk alone.

Confronting our death ultimately allows us better to live. And better to dance with God's joy amid the sorrowing nights and the hopeful mornings.

NOTES

Chapter Two

1. C. S. Lewis, *The Four Loves* (New York: Harcourt, 1960), 169.
2. Simone Weil, *Waiting for God* (New York: G. P. Putnam's, 1951), 111–112.

Chapter Three

1. *Webster's New World College Dictionary*, 4th Edition. Copyright © 2010 by Houghton Mifflin Harcourt. All rights reserved.
2. Albert Nolan, *Jesus before Christianity* (Maryknoll, N.Y.: Orbis, 1976, 1978), 32.
3. Simone Weil, *Waiting for God* (New York: G. P. Putnam's, 1951), 109–111.
4. Thomas Merton, *The Literary Essays of Thomas Merton*, ed, Brother Patrick Hart (New York: New Directions, 1981), 500.

Chapter Four

1. Arno Gruen, *The Betrayal of the Self* (New York: Grove, 1988), 281.

2. Thomas Merton, *Contemplation in a World of Action* (New York: Doubleday, 1973), 178–179.

3. L'Arche International, *Annual Summary 2020*, https://www.larche.org/documents/10181/1767074/PUB-AnnualSummary-AI-2020-EN.pdf/3ac01420-17f4-4f81-92cc-8836518a73cf.

4. Sergius Bolshakoff, *Russian Mystics* (Kalamazoo, Mich.: Cistercian, 1977), 253.

5. Martin Luther King Jr., *Strength to Love* (Philadelphia: Fortress, 1981), 47–55.

Chapter Five

1. Chaim Potok, *My Name Is Asher Lev* (New York: Knopf, 1972), 156.

ABOUT THE AUTHOR

Henri Nouwen, author, lecturer, and spiritual mentor to countless Christians around the world, was born in the Netherlands in 1932. An ordained priest and gifted teacher, he taught at several universities worldwide but spent the last decade of his life serving as pastor for the L'Arche Daybreak Community in Toronto, Canada, part of an international movement of communities that welcome people with disabilities. While on sabbatical from Daybreak, Nouwen suffered a heart attack in 1996 and died in his homeland. Nouwen's prolific writing career produced such notable works as *The Wounded Healer*, *With Open Hands*, *The Return of the Prodigal Son*, and *The Inner Voice of Love*.

TURN MY MOURNING

into

dancing

FINDING HOPE DURING
HARD TIMES

HENRI NOUWEN

COMPILED AND EDITED BY TIMOTHY JONES

W PUBLISHING GROUP

AN IMPRINT OF THOMAS NELSON

Published in Nashville, Tennessee, by W Publishing, an imprint of Thomas Nelson.

Thomas Nelson titles may be purchased in bulk for educational, business, fundraising, or sales promotional use. For information, please e-mail SpecialMarkets@ThomasNelson.com.

Scripture quotations are taken from the New Revised Standard Version Bible. Copyright © 1989 National Council of the Churches of Christ in the United States of America. Used by permission. All rights reserved worldwide.

Brief portions of chapters 1 and 2 appeared in *The New Oxford Review* under the title "The Duet of the Holy Spirit: When Mourning and Dancing Are One," June 1992 and also in *Catholic New Times*. Used by permission. The story of the trapeze artists appeared originally in *HIV/AIDS: The Second Decade* © The National Catholic AIDS Network Inc. A portion of chapter 1 first appeared in "All Is Grace," an article in *Weavings* 7:38–41 (November–December 1992). Brief passages in this book adapted from transcripts of Henri Nouwen's speeches appeared also in *The Road to Peace*, edited by John Dear and published by Orbis Books, 1988.

Editor's note: Although some of Nouwen's language might feel dated—such as the word "handicapped"—we chose to keep his original terminology, knowing his wording reflected the times in which he wrote rather than any disrespect for people with disabilities.

ISBN 978-1-4016-0377-9 (hardcover)
ISBN 978-1-4185-3609-1 (eBook)
ISBN 978-1-4016-0509-4 (audiobook)

Library of Congress Cataloging-in-Publication Data

Nouwen, Henri J. M.
Turn my mourning into dancing: moving through hard times with hope / Henri Nouwen with Timothy Jones.
p. cm.
Includes bibliographical references.
ISBN 978-0-8499-1711-0 (hc)
ISBN 978-0-8499-4509-0 (sc)
1. Grief—Religious aspects—Christianity. 2. Consolation. I. Jones, Timothy K., 1955–II. Title.
BV4905.3 .N68 2001
242'.4—dc21   2001045620

Printed in the United States of America

22 23 24 25 26 LSC 10 9 8 7 6 5 4 3 2 1